HUMANISTS
AND JURISTS

SIX STUDIES IN
THE RENAISSANCE

HUMANISTS AND JURISTS

SIX STUDIES IN THE RENAISSANCE

MYRON P. GILMORE

THE BELKNAP PRESS OF

HARVARD UNIVERSITY PRESS

CAMBRIDGE, MASSACHUSETTS

1963

DEDICATED TO

MY CHILDREN

PREFACE

T H E following studies are all concerned with varying aspects of the appearance during the Italian Renaissance of new ideas on the nature and function of history. These ideas included a new perspective on the past, a new method for interpreting the meaning of documents of the past, and a reformulation of the traditional doctrine that history was philosophy teaching by example. Humanists and lawyers were closely linked in the development of a historical method and the application of its results to the understanding of the present. The intellectual interests of the lawyers had already had a formative influence on the pre-Petrarchan humanist circles in Padua and Mantua. Petrarch who had himself spent seven years in the study of the law was contemptuous of the traditional methods of teaching and exposition. In spite of his indictment it was in the end the best of the legal scholars who applied Petrarch's ideas and most fully developed the consequences of a historical understanding grounded on the philological analysis of a text. The essay on the lawyers and the Church contains some examples of the application to the ecclesiastical scene in the early sixteenth century of ideas derived by the humanist jurists from their study of law and history.

Erasmus was the heir of the Italian humanists and

appropriated in his own thought their historical conquest of the classical and early Christian worlds. To him two studies are devoted, the first an explicit discussion of his conception of history and the second an analysis of the consequences of his views for the general position taken in the last years of his life. Erasmus's rejection of the Reformation was in large part conditioned by the ideas on history and on rhetoric developed by the Italian fifteenth-century educators. His greatest friend and heir, Boniface Amerbach, the subject of the last essay, provides an example in his career and in his thought of an initial enthusiastic acceptance of the new historical methods for the understanding of both law and religion, followed, however, by a sense of disillusionment with the consequences. In a sense, therefore, Amerbach in his relation to Erasmus brings to a close a chapter which had begun nearly two hundred years before with Petrarch's letter to a young friend in Genoa, counselling him against the study of the law.

Of the studies here assembled, portions or versions of four have been previously published. I am grateful to the several publishers for permission to reprint them here. "The Renaissance Conception of the Lessons of History" was one of the lectures given on the Arensberg Foundation at the University of Southern California. These were published in 1959 under the title *Facets of the Renaissance* by the University of Southern California Press. This lecture has been rewritten and much enlarged. A large part of the text of "Individualism in Renaissance Historians" appeared under the title "Freedom and Determinism in Renaissance Historians" in *Studies in the Renais-*

PREFACE

sance (Renaissance Society of America, 1956), III, 49–60. It, also, has undergone extensive changes and additions. "The Lawyers and the Church in the Italian Renaissance" was presented as a lecture at the Rice Institute in 1959 and was published without documentation in *The Rice Institute Pamphlet* 46 (1960). Notes have been supplied and new material added. "Fides et Eruditio: Erasmus and the Study of History" was included in *Teachers of History: Essays in Honor of Laurence Bradford Packard* (Cornell University Press, 1954). A new section on Valla has been appended in the concluding pages. The final two studies, "Erasmus and the Cause of Christian Humanism" and "Boniface Amerbach," have not previously appeared in print. The former, however, was given as a public lecture at the University of Texas and at the Program for Christian Culture, St. Mary's College, Notre Dame, Indiana.

I am particularly indebted to Dr. Hans Baron and Professor Guido Kisch. Dr. Baron read the entire manuscript critically; Professor Kisch, the chapter on Amerbach.

My daughter, Diana Gilmore, shared the burden of proofreading and is responsible for making the index.

I desire to express my gratitude to the Guggenheim Foundation and to the Fulbright Commission for grants which enabled me to spend the year 1956–1957 in Europe where the material for some of these essays was gathered.

Myron P. Gilmore

July 21, 1963

CONTENTS

ILLUSTRATIONS

꧁ ꧂

The woodcut of Erasmus with Terminus is reproduced from the proof in the collection of Mr. and Mrs. Philip Hofer of Cambridge, Massachusetts, by their kind permission.

The portraits of Petrarch, Alciato, Valla, Decio, and Maino are reproduced from J. J. Boissard, *Biblitheca sive thesaurus virtutis et gloriae in quo continentur illustrium eruditione et doctrina virorum effigies et vitae summa diligentia accurate descriptae et in centurias duas distributae* (Frankfort, 1628), through the courtesy of the Houghton Library, Harvard University. These portraits should not be considered as historical likenesses but were probably

ILLUSTRATIONS

taken from iconographic types. The same features were frequently used with different headdresses and robes to represent different individuals. Such portraits, however, are interesting in that they indicate how the sixteenth century visualized the cultural heroes of a past age.

The portraits of Cujas and Bartolus are reproduced from the frontispieces of their collected works, respectively *Opera omnia*, ed. Alexander Scot (Lyons, 1606) and *Opera omnia* (Basel, 1589), through the courtesy of the Treasure Room of the Harvard Law Library.

Guillaume Budé's portrait is reproduced from André Thevet, *Les vrais pourtraits et vies des hommes illustres, grecz, latins, et payens, recueilliz de leur tableaux, livres, medalles, antiques et modernes* (Paris, 1584), through the courtesy of the Houghton Library, Harvard University.

The portrait of Zasius is reproduced from Nicholas Reusner, *Icones sive imagines virorum letteris illustrium* (Strasbourg, 1590), through the courtesy of the Houghton Library, Harvard University.

The two portraits of Amerbach are reproduced from the original paintings in the Kunstmuseum, Basel, with the kind permission of the Director.

HUMANISTS AND JURISTS

SIX STUDIES IN THE RENAISSANCE

I

THE RENAISSANCE
CONCEPTION OF THE
LESSONS OF HISTORY

❧ ❧

O N E of the keys to the understanding of the mentality
of a past epoch is to be found in the study of its ideas
about history. What men think about the past tells us
also a good deal of what they think about the present.
Perhaps the most important distinction between primitive
and civilized societies is that, in the former, the memory
of events in earlier generations is not differentiated, while,
in the latter, a sense of the past adds a dimension to present
existence. A man may react first of all to the similarities
and even uniformities which unite his experience to that
of his ancestors, or, on the other hand, he may be most
impressed by the contrast between his and his great-grand-
father's situation, but in either case he transcends his own
immediate environment; in Becker's phrase, he enlarges
his "specious present." [1] Whether he looks at change or
continuity, the result of considering the past is in some
sense a lesson of history. The effort to understand the past
may fluctuate between the search for uniformities and
the appreciation of the unique, but in either case history
is an educative process in the literal sense of leading a man

[1] Carl Becker, "Everyman His Own Historian," *American Historical
Review* 37:221–236 (1931–1932). See especially p. 226.

[1]

out of himself. It provides an enlargement of the horizon and discloses an infinite variety of views. Decisions about what part of the landscape to study and how to study it are conditioned not only by the personality of the observer but more subtly by the civilization, period, generation, or social group to which he belongs.

It is obvious that different civilizations have entertained very different ideas of time and the historical process. The historical works of any epoch are in fact as much conditioned by the general "style" of the period in which they are produced as are the creations of architecture, sculpture, and painting. We are all familiar—perhaps too familiar— with the contrasts between oriental and occidental conceptions of time and, within Western history, between the Greek idea of recurrence and the Hebrew idea of linear development. The Greeks, it is said, knew phenomena which had a beginning and an end and also those which had no beginning and no end, but they had no conception either of an act of creation which brought a universe into existence or of an absolutely unique event occupying the place of the Incarnation in Christian history. We find another familiar example of the differences between modes of historical interpretation in the contrast between the medieval providential view of history and the doctrine of progress which was elaborated in the eighteenth century and has flourished until the shocks of the twentieth. These are illustrations on the most comprehensive scale, but, even within the "subperiods" in the history of modern Western civilization, changes in the conception of the meaning of history have been characteristic of the successive stages in the intellectual development of Europe.

In periods of stability and peace history recedes into a distant background. In Victorian England history was generally considered to have stopped at the Battle of Waterloo in 1815, but, in the twentieth century, it is a usual feeling that we are only too much caught up in the historical process. By the traditional division that still prevails in most European countries *histoire moderne* commences with the Renaissance or Reformation and finishes with 1789, whereas *histoire contemporaine* still begins with the French Revolution. The estimates of what constitutes "history" as opposed to "present" have fluctuated with the even more varied value judgments on the relation of past to present. From the time of the Greeks there have been some generations who have turned back to a golden age in the past and endowed a primitive society with all the virtues and none of the vices of civilization.[2] Others, however, have looked on primitive society as one in which all life was, in Hobbes's famous phrase, "solitary, poor, nasty, brutish, and short." Some philosophers in the nineteenth century regarded their own age as the culmination of the historical process while others measured their own times against an idealized period in the past, the great age of Greece or the thirteenth "greatest of centuries," and found in the comparison only grounds for despair.

These contrasts, between progress and decadence, between evolution and recurrence, between optimism and pessimism, have fixed the bounds within which the West-

---

[2] For a survey of attitudes toward primitive society see A. O. Lovejoy and George Boas, *Primitivism and Related Ideas in Antiquity* (Baltimore, 1935).

ern tradition has elaborated its ideas on the meaning of history. In this long and complex evolution a significant stage is marked by the period of the Renaissance in which there appeared a new and distinctive attitude toward historical studies.

The concept of the Renaissance has given rise to much controversy and a voluminous literature.[3] The metaphor was originally invoked to describe certain intellectual and artistic achievements, first in Italy and subsequently in the rest of Europe, in the period from the fourteenth to the seventeenth century, but modern usage has popularized its application to the period as a whole. In spite of the vague and multiple meanings which the term has in consequence acquired, it has become deeply embedded in our historical vocabulary. In general, it is applied with more precision to intellectual rather than to institutional history, using the term intellectual in its broadest sense, and this is the more justifiable because the great changes of the period were in the realm of the arts and the mind and not in political and economic life.[4] The latter was far from static but, viewing the European scene as a whole, it cannot be said that the Renaissance saw transformations in institutions which matched in anything like the same degree those in the history of ideas. The intellectual revolution was profound, and was both cause and conse-

[3] Perhaps the best introduction to the present state of the question and the bibliography is the essay by F. Chabod, "The Concept of the Renaissance," in *Machiavelli and the Renaissance* (Cambridge, Mass., 1959), pp. 149–247.

[4] An effective statement of this view is contained in H. Trevor-Roper, "The General Crisis of the Seventeenth Century," *Past and Present*, no. 16 (November 1959), pp. 31–64.

quence of the enormous extension of knowledge and experience in time and space. Greek and Roman history, and especially the latter, came into ever clearer view and the increasing knowledge of classical civilization posed anew the problem of the relation between classical and Christian values. The mass of information brought back to Europe by travellers and missionaries in the sixteenth century created an analogous problem on the relation of contemporary non-Christian civilizations to that of western Europe. The exploration of antiquity preceded the exploration of Asia and the new world, and it is in fourteenth-century Italy that we find the first consciously held, new attitudes toward the classical past. In the elaboration of these attitudes, as in so many other areas, Petrarch was a figure of commanding importance, and any description of the historical ideas of the Italian Renaissance must begin with a consideration of his thought.

In many of his works Petrarch reveals a preoccupation with time and the position of his own age in relation to the past and to the future. This is perhaps most dramatically apparent in the series of letters addressed to ancient authors in the last book of the *Familiares*. In these compositions Petrarch wrote to his favorite literary heroes in antiquity in the tone he used in writing to his friends in his own age. It was an imaginative effort to cross the centuries that separated the classical authors from Petrarch and it was predicated on a real apprehension of the remoteness of the ancient world. The intensity of the longing together with the realization of the impossibility of its fulfillment created the conditions for these extraordinary communications.

In the letter to Livy Petrarch begins with the wish that he had been born in Livy's age or Livy in his. They would have been able to console each other. Petrarch bewails the destruction of the lost books and says that he resorts to reading Livy whenever he wishes to forget the conditions of Italy and the moral standards of his own time. "I am filled with bitter indignation," he writes, "against the mores of today when men value nothing except gold and silver and desire nothing except sensual pleasures." He is grateful to Livy for permitting him to forget the present evils and, as if closing a conversation which he had really had but which he can never have again, he concludes with the apostrophe: "Farewell forever, O matchless historian!" The letter is significantly dated, "Written in the land of the living, in that part of Italy and in that city in which I am now living and where you were once born and buried, in the vestibule of the temple of Justina Virgo, and in view of your very tombstone on the twenty-second of February, and in the thirteenth hundred and fiftieth year from the birth of him whom you would have seen or of whose birth you would have heard, had you lived a little longer." [5] Four of the other epistles in this group contain in their dating similar references to the pre-Christian era. The letter to Cicero is written "in the thirteen hundred and forty-fifth year of that God whom you never knew"; that to Quintilian "in the thirteen hundred and fiftieth year from the birth of him whom your master preferred to persecute rather than profess." [6]

[5] Petrarch, *Epistolae de rebus familiaribus et variae,* J. Fracassetti, ed., 3 vols. (Florence, 1859–1863), III, 282. My translation.
[6] *Ibid.,* pp. 263, 280.

These expressions show not only that Petrarch was acutely conscious of the distance which separated him from his admired classical authors but also that he realized psychologically at least something of what it meant to live before the Christian era. It does not matter that he was wrong in many of the details of his historical and architectural reconstructions—we now know, for example, that he was not looking at the actual tomb of Livy at Padua[7]—but it is significant that these phrases in which he dates his letters and places his own position in time reveal the working of an historical imagination. Petrarch knew that Livy knew nothing of Christianity, although he would have heard of it had he lived a little longer; he knew also that Quintilian had been employed by the Emperor Domitian who persecuted the Christians. But with this knowledge he was able to imagine what these facts meant; he was able to some extent to place the lives and works of these authors in the context of their times. It is not too much to say that he had some conception of anachronism and that this conception underlay his understanding of the fact that no knowledge of Christianity could be attributed to Livy.

We are today so accustomed to applying the test of anachronism to our historical reconstructions that we take it for granted. Every schoolboy knows that Roman senators did not smoke cigars and that Napoleon's troops did not fight with machine guns. The wide diffusion of knowledge about what belongs in particular historical periods does not, of course, prevent the frequent occur-

[7] B. L. Ullman, "The Post-Mortem Adventures of Livy," in *Studies in the Italian Renaissance* (Rome, 1955), pp. 55–79.

rence of amusing mistakes. The historical novelist who described a moving scene of farewell between father and son in 1356 when the latter declared his intention of going "to fight in the Hundred Years War" forgot that the war could have been so christened only by a later generation.[8] But, on the whole, we are more conscious than any previous civilization of the succession of historical epochs and of the differences between them. We know that if we are going to construct Colonial Williamsburg as it really was, the streets must be cobbled and the electric wires put under ground. It might indeed be said that in such extreme cases of stage-set reconstruction we commit anachronisms in reverse by requiring modern stores to encase themselves in Queen Anne or Georgian fronts. The very phrase "to commit an anachronism" is furthermore a reminder of the extent to which we think of the concept in pejorative terms. An anachronism is a bad thing. Anachronisms in films, novels, legal, and administrative systems are pointed out to be condemned. Anthony Wedgwood Benn in England, appealing to the High Court to be allowed to divest himself of his hereditary peerage, argued that the condition which prevents his being in the House of Commons is an anachronism that ought to be corrected.[9] The very success of our historical reconstructions, the triumphs of a sense of history, have led us to apply to the realm of ideas the same arguments that are used in determining the "period" of furniture, clothes, architecture, or details of daily life. We would all agree with Sir Isaiah Berlin that Hamlet could

[8] I owe this reference to Professor B. J. Whiting.
[9] *The New York Times,* July 29, 1961.

not have been written at the court of Genghis Khan and that anyone who asserts it was is not only mistaken but mad.[10] Yet we often too confidently assert that a particular idea could not have been entertained (because it would have been an anachronism) in the Renaissance, or the Enlightenment, or the Victorian era. However certain we may be of our conclusions about the physical environment in history and about the artifacts which have been created by men, we must in the end recognize that there have always been and always will be human anachronisms and this is, in fact, one of the conditions that prevents the course of history from being as determined as some philosophers have supposed.

This overdeveloped modern consciousness is the product of a long evolution which may be said to have begun with Petrarch and those of his followers who shared his attitude toward the past. The conception of history which prevailed in the Middle Ages was one of a course of events extending from the creation in the past to the last judgment in the future. Within this unified Christian drama there was small scope for the realization of or interest in the differences that divided one period from another, and consequently no conception of anachronism.[11] In the history of art Professor Panofsky has pointed out the divorce in the Middle Ages between classical form and classical content. Those who worked from literary sources represented ancient gods and goddesses or Greek and Trojan heroes in medieval costumes, whereas the artists

[10] I. Berlin, "History and Theory: The Concept of Scientific History," *History and Theory: Studies in the Philosophy of History* 1:5 (1960).
[11] Eva M. Sanford, "The Study of Ancient History in the Middle Ages," *Journal of the History of Ideas* 5:21–43 (1944).

who drew on visual materials dressed Christian figures in classical drapery.[12] Petrarch's attitude represents a decisive change from this medieval way of looking at the past. His letter to Livy puts Livy back into the Roman past in a way which is entirely different from the illustrator of the fourteenth-century French manuscript of Livy who represented the scenes of Roman history as if they were taking place in the France or Burgundy of his own day. The very idea of what is anachronistic, that is, something which is out of its own proper time, whether it is a detail of costume, an idea, an event, or a linguistic expression, rests on a sense of the differences that separate one historical epoch from another. This sense of difference between the present and various periods of the past was, of course, not as sharp as it later became; we are still far from the historicism of the nineteenth and twentieth centuries. In the drama and the arts anachronisms were not regarded as offensive until after the conquests of romanticism. Yet, incomplete as it was, the Renaissance had some sense of the life and style of the past. The humanist followers of Petrarch used the argument from anachronism among others as a weapon of historical criticism.[13] Conversely the

[12] Erwin Panofsky, *Renaissance and Renascences in Western Art* (Stockholm, 1961). See especially ch. ii, pp. 42–133; also the author's earlier article "Renaissance and Renascences," *The Kenyon Review* 6:201–306 (1944).

[13] For example, Lorenzo Valla in his *De falso credita et ementita Constantini donatione,* W. Schwahn, ed. (Berlin, 1927). See p. 44: "Iste non putat illud nisi ex auro esse, cui circulus aureus nunc cum gemmis apponi a regibus solet." There is a discussion of Valla as a historian in F. Gaeta, *Lorenzo Valla: Filologia e storia dell'umanesimo Italiano* (Naples, 1955) pp. 129–192. Gaeta's view of Valla's significance is criticized by Hanna H. Gray, "History and Rhetoric in Quattrocento Humanism" (unpub. diss., Radcliffe College, 1957), especially in ch. iv.

recovery of a sense of classical "style" made possible the imitation of ancient works of art and literature; we remember that Michelangelo's first sculpture was sold as a Roman marble and Alberti circulated a comedy he had written as a newly found work of Latin literature.[14]

Petrarch's appreciation of the relation between his own time and the classical past led him also to an interest in projecting the present into the future. One result of this interest is the celebrated letter to posterity. In this epistle he speaks directly to us as he had spoken to Livy and the other classical authors: "Greeting. It is possible that some word of me may have come to you, though even this is doubtful, since an insignificant and obscure name will scarcely penetrate far in either time or space. If, however, you should have heard of me, you may desire to know what manner of man I was ..." [15] The charming description of Petrarch's physical qualities which follows and the account of his emotional and intellectual development show his desire to project accurate information on himself as an individual to the remotest generations. It may indeed be said that both the letters to ancient authors and the letter to posterity show the same interest in preserving from the distortions of time some portion of the truth.

Petrarch's preoccupation with the destructiveness of time found its most powerful expression in the *Trionfi*. In these allegories which open with the triumph of Love,

[14] On Michelangelo, see Charles De Tolnay, *The Youth of Michelangelo* (Princeton, 1947), p. 27 and note 88. On Alberti, see G. Mancini, *Vita di Leon Battista Alberti* (Florence, 1911), pp. 54–55.

[15] The latest and best edition of this letter is in Petrarch, *Prose,* G. Martellotti, ed. (Milan, 1955), pp. 2–19. The quotation is from the English translation by James H. Robinson in *Petrarch: The First Modern Man* (New York, 1909), p. 59.

Chastity triumphs over Love, Death over Chastity, Fame over Death, Time over Fame, and, finally, Eternity over Time. The famous names of history are poisoned by time; lordships and kingdoms fail; time cuts off all that is mortal.

> Vidi ogni nostra gloria, al Sol, di neve . . .

> Tanto vince e ritoglie il Tempo avaro;
>   Chiamasi Fama, ed e morir secondo;
>   Ne piu che contra il primo e alcun riparo.

> Cosi il Temp trionfa i nomi e'l mondo.[16]

In spite of the ultimate or, rather, penultimate victory of Time (since Time is in the end itself conquered by Eternity), it was yet possible for mortals to rescue from time those records of experience which had been preserved by eloquence. It was even possible to recover works which had been lost in the darkness of time as Petrarch had himself found the manuscripts of Cicero's letters to Atticus. The consciousness of the difference between his own time and republican Rome—the sense of historical perspective—was accompanied in Petrarch's thought by a revaluation of the traditional judgments on Roman history. The age about which Livy wrote in the third decade of his history, even the age in which Cicero had lived, appeared clearly to Petrarch's vision as, in some important respects, better than the present, and this in spite of the fact that it lacked the benefit of Christian revelation. In the letter to Livy, as well as in many of his other works, Petrarch approaches the conception of a culturally "dark" or middle age lying between his own time and antiquity,

[16] Petrarch, *I Trionfi* (Florence, 1908), pp. 105–106.

a conception which has been so familiar a feature of the periodization of history from the Renaissance to the present time.[17]

Even in the arena of political life Petrarch at times thought it possible to apply conceptions resurrected from this Roman past. The most dramatic occasion on which he intervened was the ill-starred revolt of Rienzo in Rome in 1347. Niccola or Cola di Rienzo was the son of a notary whose imagination had been powerfully affected by what he knew of Roman history and what he saw of Roman ruins. He had discovered an inscription of the *lex regia* by which it was declared that the *populus* had given over to the emperor all its *imperium et potestas*. His opportunity came when he was sent on a mission to the papal court at Avignon where he was able to establish relations with Petrarch on whom his fervent oratory and appeals to the Roman past made a strong impression. Returning to Rome he was able to put himself at the head of a revolutionary movement directed against the domination of the nobility. In a burst of patriotic fervor he declared himself "Nicholas the severe and clement, Tribune of liberty, peace, and justice, liberator of the sacred Roman Republic and illustrious prefect of the mother city." In a series of pompous communications to the cities and rulers of Italy and to the pope he announced the restoration of Roman liberty under his rule and the assumption by Rome of the position to which her cultural and political heritage entitled her.[18]

[17] See T. Mommsen, "Petrarch's Conception of the Dark Ages," *Speculum* 17:226–249 (1943).

[18] On Rienzo, see Paul Piur, *Cola di Rienzo* (Milan, 1934), and Iris Origo, *Tribune of Rome: A Biography of Cola di Rienzo* (London,

Petrarch was stirred to generous enthusiasm by Rienzo's program and wrote eloquent epistles to Rienzo and to the Roman people. Carried away by his own rhetoric, in one of these communications, he hails Rienzo as the reincarnation of Romulus, Brutus, and Camillus. "Hail! Author of Roman liberty, Roman peace and Roman tranquility! To you the present generation owes the fact that it will be able to die in liberty and posterity the fact that it will be born in liberty." [19] This letter was followed by an eclogue addressed to Rienzo and voicing Petrarch's hopes in a similar manner.[20] Thus, the evils of Petrarch's own time were condemned by the standards exhibited by the ancient Romans. Petrarch's appeal to the Roman past reflected the conviction that history, even pagan history, provided a basis for moral criticism. Insofar as the examples of virtue and vice furnished by the past could be imitated and actively realized in the present, history was philosophy teaching by example.

This conception is apparent not only in Petrarch's interventions in active political life which were rather rare, but also in his own historical compositions. His collection of biographies, *De viris illustribus,* was originally conceived to include epitomes of the lives of great men which Petrarch had found scattered through history books. In the final version, composed in the last years of his life

---

1938). Rienzo's correspondence has been edited with an extensive commentary by Konrad Burdach in *Vom Mittelalter zur Reformation: Forschungen zur Geschichte der Deutschen Bildung,* vol. II, pt. III: *Briefwechsel des Cola di Rienzo.* The quoted declaration is published on pp. 100–106 of this volume. My translation.

[19] Burdach, ed., *Briefwechsel des Cola di Rienzo,* p. 95.
[20] *Ibid.,* pp. 87–93.

at the request of the tyrant Francesco da Carrara, Petrarch returned to his first plan of concentrating entirely on Roman lives, in accordance with the preference expressed by the prince, who proposed to decorate a hall of his palace with the portraits of the subjects of Petrarch's biographies.[21] His preference for the Romans again shows his sense of the division which separated classical and early Christian antiquity from the dark ages that followed after. He had earlier expressed his reluctance to include any contemporary or recent figures in his collection of illustrious lives. In a letter to Agapito Colonna written in 1359 he says, in answer to the charge that he did not include in his biographical collection any contemporary figures, "I did not wish to guide my pen so far and through such darkness." [22] Even, however, when Petrarch did turn to this "darkness" for historical and biographical material, his purpose remained didactic. *Rerum memorandarum libri* were composed to illustrate a traditional conception of virtue derived from Cicero.[23] According to this tradition, prudence, one of the four cardinal virtues was divided into three parts, the memory of things past, the consciousness of things present, and the foreseeing of things to come. The individuals selected to illustrate these different aspects of prudence are divided into Roman, non-Roman, and modern, although the greater number by far is Roman and illustrates again Petrarch's belief in

[21] E. H. Wilkins, *Petrarch's Later Years* (Cambridge, Mass., 1959), pp. 283–302.

[22] *Epistolae*, III, 30–31. Quoted by T. Mommsen, "Petrarch's Conception of the Dark Ages," *Speculum* 17:226–249 (1942).

[23] *Rerum memorandarum libri*, G. Billanovich, ed. (Florence, 1945), introduction, pp. cixxiv–cxxx.

the superiority of Roman history as a source of moral examples.

In spite of the didactic purpose of Petrarch's formal historical and biographical work, it must not, however, be forgotten that there was another aspect of his historical interests which in the end was of far greater importance for European historiography. This is his appeal for a return to the sources, *ad fontes,* and his concern for what an ancient author had really said. In his treatise *On His Own Ignorance* he condemns "the stupid Aristotelians, who day by day in every single word they speak do not cease to hammer into the heads of others Aristotle whom they know by name only." [24] A great part of Petrarch's career was dedicated to his attempt to recover the accurate texts of his beloved classical authors. If he was convinced that the history of Livy provided examples for the present, he was equally convinced that it was necessary to know precisely what Livy had said, so far as this was possible, after the destruction wrought by time and barbarians. We have only recently come to know, through the researches of Professor Billanovich, how much Petrarch contributed to the establishment of the text of Livy.[25] Petrarch early copied one of the most important manuscripts of Livy, now known as the Harleian at Oxford, and dedicated himself to the reconstruction of the best possible text. "The tradition of Livy duing the Renaissance," says Professor Billanovich, "was for the most part

---

[24] Petrarch, "On His Own Ignorance," Hans Nachod, tr., in *The Renaissance Philosophy of Man,* P. O. Kristeller and J. H. Randall, Jr., eds. (Chicago, 1945), p. 107.

[25] G. Billanovich, "Petrarch and the Textual Tradition of Livy," *Journal of the Warburg Institute* 14:125 ff. (1951).

the tradition which Petrarch himself had formed. By means of a fortunate comparison of texts, he corrected the books of the first *Decade;* which, although descended from a single archetype, had been transmitted through divergent channels. And he managed to obtain the fourth *Decade* when it had only just reached Avignon." [26] Throughout his life Livy remained for Petrarch his favorite historian.

It may be pointed out that this effort to establish with the aid of grammar and philology what Livy or another ancient author had really written stopped a good deal short of what we understand by historical research. For Petrarch Livy *was* Roman history and there was no question of going behind his narrative to investigate what had actually happened through a process of comparing different documents and different kinds of evidence.[27] Nevertheless, the attempt to recover a correct text did involve coming into more direct contact with the character, personality, style, and idiosyncracies of the author—Livy was felt as a more real historical personage—than had been the case in the middle ages.[28] Furthermore, the comparison of two or more manuscripts was at least the beginning of criticism even if the scope was limited to the recovery of one narrative history rather than the reconstruction of a past through the testimony of many.[29]

[26] *Ibid.,* p. 172.
[27] Cf. Hanna H. Gray, unpub. diss., especially ch. iv.
[28] On the "taking contact" with the personalities of the past, see E. Garin, "La storia nel pensiero del rinascimento," in *Medioevo e Rinascimento* (Bari, 1954), pp. 194–210, especially p. 204.
[29] On the use of critical methods by humanist historians, see B. Ullman, "Leonardo Bruni and Humanist Historiography," *Studies in the Renaissance* (Rome, 1955), pp. 321–344.

There may thus be distinguished in Petrarch's attitude toward history three different components. There is first the sense of historical distance, the consciousness of the differences between classical antiquity and the Christian era, followed by dawning realization that this great gap in time and circumstances could be bridged by an effort of the imagination. Secondly, there is the conception that to the extent to which this past can be recovered it provides moral lessons for a future generation. History is philosophy teaching by example in which the past, if correctly understood, informs and instructs the present. Thirdly, there is the basis for that correct understanding, that is, history as the conquest of what an ancient author had really said, derived from a critical and philological study of the texts. Our modern habits of thought about history tend in general to make a sharp separation between these latter two components. Much that may be discovered by research is irrelevant to any "lessons" of history and conversely many moral and political "truths" cannot be supported by historical evidence, or, at any rate, by historical evidence alone. In the minds of Petrarch and his immediate followers, however, there cannot be said to have been any sense of incompatibility between these two components of the historian's activity. For most of the characteristic thinkers of the Renaissance the cry for the return to the sources was accompanied by the conviction that the sources when recovered would be relevant to present concerns. Criticism and a program for moral and educational reform sustained each other, and until they began to be separated provided the basis of the hopes of the humanist publicists.

The intellectual impulse given by Petrarch to historical

studies can be traced in succeeding generations. Editions and translations of ancient historians were produced in increasing numbers and many humanists wrote histories modelled on Livy. The study of history was elevated to an important and sometimes to a central position in the educational curriculum. The Florentine chancellor, Coluccio Salutati, one of Petrarch's great admirers, wrote in 1392 a letter to the Grand Master of the Order of St. John of Jerusalem praising him for his valuable collection of books. Among these he singled out for particular mention the histories, and he commended the Grand Master for having "cherished the historians whose duty it is to hand down to posterity the memory of things done so that the examples of kings, nations, and illustrious men can be either equalled or exceeded by imitating them . . . The knowledge of things done warns princes, teaches people, and instructs individuals . . . It is the most certain basis for the conduct of affairs. History teaches us the doctrines of philosophy. What is rhetoric itself, one of the most beautiful of the sciences, but the conflict and opposition between things which have been done and things which ought to have been done?" [30] Salutati's emphasis on rhetoric is significant. The claims of rhetoric against the position of medieval dialectic were one of the means by which the humanists strove to advance their cause. Only through the genius of eloquence exercised in the arrangement and disposition of the material could historians save events and individuals from the ravages of time and make fully effective the lessons to be learned.[31]

[30] Salutati, *Epistolario di Coluccio Salutati*, F. Novati, ed. (Rome, 1891–1905), II, 289–295. My translation.
[31] See Hanna H. Gray's discussion of the relation between history and rhetoric.

The judgment of Salutati was confirmed by the formal treatises on education. Pier Paolo Vergerio, for example, whose *De ingenuis moribus* is of the beginning of the fifteenth century, declares in his discussion of the ideal curriculum: "We come now to the consideration of the various subjects which ought to be included under the name of liberal studies. Among these I accord the first place to history on the grounds both of its attractiveness and its utility, qualities which appeal equally to the scholar and the statesman . . . History, then gives us the concrete examples of the principles inculcated by philosophy. The one shows what men should do, the other what men have said and done in the past and what practical lessons men may draw therefrom for the present day." [32] Such a text as this clearly reveals the consequences of Petrarch's approach to historical studies: there was no gulf between the study and the market place, no divorce between culture and politics.

The most celebrated Italian historian of the first part of the fifteenth century affirmed the same ideas in both his life and his work. As Florentine chancellor and successor to Salutati, Leonardo Bruni endeavored to put into practice the lessons on civic liberty which he, as a scholar, had learned from Roman history.[33] He believed that he

[32] P. P. Vergerio, *De ingenuis moribus et liberalibus studiis adolescentiae*, A. Onesotto, ed. (Padua, 1918), p. 121. English translation by W. W. Woodward, *Vittorino da Feltre and Other Renaissance Educators* (Cambridge, Eng., 1918), p. 106.

[33] See, for the most thorough discussion of the ideas of Bruni and his circle, the two-volume work by Hans Baron, *The Crisis of the Early Italian Renaissance: Civic Humanism and Republican Liberty in an Age of Classicism and Tyranny* (Princeton, 1955), especially vol. I, pp. 163–240.

ought to leave behind him a history of his own epoch so that future generations could draw from it the same kind of lessons as he had drawn from the study of the classical world. "I feel that I have an obligation," he wrote at the beginning of his *Rerum suorum tempore gestarum*, "to this age of mine, to give some notice of it to posterity in whatsoever light it may appear to the future. If only those who lived before us and who had some literary ability had done this, we would not today find ourselves in such a state of darkness and ignorance. Indeed it appears to me that the age of Cicero and Demosthenes are much better known than that of sixty years ago." [34] Thus Bruni combined an effort to extend his knowledge of the past with the exaltation of the lessons which had been learned from Roman history. In developing further the periodization which had been suggested by Petrarch he bore witness to the sense of emergence from a time of darkness which was so characteristic of many of his contemporaries. [35]

These views on history and particularly on Roman history as a source of moral example were adopted by educators. Most influential among those who founded new schools or reformed the traditional curricula was Vittorino da Feltre, the beloved schoolmaster of Mantua. Vittorino had been educated in the full tide of enthusiasm for grammar, rhetoric, history, poetry, and moral philosophy as against logic, dialectic, and natural philosophy. He revolted against the moral and intellectual tone of the

---

[34] Leonardo Bruni, *Rerum suo tempore gestarum commentarius,* Carmine di Pierro, ed., in the new edition of *Rerum Italicarum Scriptores,* vol. XIX, pt. 3 (Citta di Castello, 1914), p. 423.

[35] See B. L. Ullman, "Leonardo Bruni and Humanist Historiography," in *Studies in the Italian Renaissance* (Rome, 1955), pp. 321–344.

University of Padua, where he taught for a time, and subsequently opened his own school in Venice. Thence he was summoned to Mantua by the Marquis Gonzaga who entrusted to Vittorino the education of his children. The *Casa Giocosa,* established in a Gonzaga villa, became the model for educational reform and for the fullest development of the program of the early humanists. Among its pupils were to be found the children of poor families as well as the princes of the house of Gonzaga. Vittorino was also an innovator in providing equal opportunities for girls and boys. The ideals of his program reflected a fusion of classic and Christian traditions; he inculcated above all the precepts of service to the state and society whether in the active life of a statesman or in the contemplative life of a religious vocation. He won the affectionate devotion of all his pupils and perhaps the monument which best characterizes his achievement is the medal of Pisanello with the sensitive portrait and the inscription, "Summus mathematicus et omnis humanitatis pater." On the obverse of the medal is the representation of a pelican opening its breast to feed its young, a traditional symbol of sacrifice.[36]

In this school a great importance was accorded to the study of history and Livy remained always, for Vittorino as he had been for Petrarch, one of the most cherished authors. The pupils learned to read aloud and memorize passages from Livy and they discussed the heroes of Roman history in the spirit in which Petrarch had collected his exemplary

---

[36] On Vittorino and his school, see W. W. Woodward, *Vittorino da Feltre,* and E. Garin, *L'educazione in Europa (1400–1600)* (Bari, 1957), pp. 147–153.

biographies. The results of this education can be followed in the later lives of two of his pupils, Giovanni Andrea Bussi, Bishop of Aleria, and Federico da Montefeltro, Duke of Urbino.

The Bishop of Aleria in Corsica served four popes as acolyte, secretary, and librarian, and although he was rewarded with two Corsican bishoprics, Alessio and Aleria, he never visited his sees. He enjoys the remarkable distinction of having collaborated with the first Roman printers, Sweynheim and Pannartz at Subiaco and at Rome, in the publishing of the *editiones principes* of a large number of Latin authors including Livy.[37] In the preface to the Livy of 1469 he traces his first acquaintance with Livy to Vittorino's school and professes that he owes most of his knowledge of the text to Vittorino, who had been the first to introduce him to Petrarch's work on Livy. He pays touching tribute to Vittorino as the "Socrates of our age," and as "sapientiae magister, honestatis specimen, bonitatis exemplus, divitiarum contemptor." [38] This famous edition, appearing within five years of the centenary of the death of Petrarch, is an eloquent testimony to the fruit of Petrarch's interest in the text of Livy. By an invention of which Petrarch could not even have dreamed his textual reconstruction, which had descended to Vittorino and to Valla, was now reproduced in a manner which would make it available to all readers and scholars.

[37] On Andrea Bussi, see *Enciclopedia Italiana* (Milan, 1929–), art. "Bussi," and H. Quentin, *Essais de critique textuelle* (Paris, 1926), p. 27 ff.

[38] Livy, *Historiae Romanae Decades,* G. Andrea, ed. (Rome, 1469), preface.

The most famous pupil of Vittorino was Federigo da Montefeltro, Count and subsequently Duke of Urbino. Federigo, whose profile with the nicked nose is familiar to us from many contemporary portraits, offers the ideal example of the Renaissance prince. He distinguished himself at an early age as a military strategist and commander of men, and he served as various times in the employ of Venice, Florence, and the papacy as well as fighting his own battles. As a ruler he organized in his territories an efficient administration and provided justice for his subjects. As a patron of arts and letters he built the great ducal palace at Urbino, a most perfect example of fifteenth-century domestic architecture, and employed for its decoration the most gifted artists he could find. To fill his library he commissioned the Florentine bookseller Vespasiano da Bisticci to hire an army of copyists to make the beautiful manuscripts of the Greek, Roman, and Christian classics that he wished to possess.[39] Although as a youth he had studied for only two years at Vittorino's school, he never forgot his master and in the study at the ducal palace where were enshrined portraits of the worthies of all ages there was included Berruguete's portrait of Vittorino with an inscription recording the gratitude of the duke. It was undoubtedly in Vittorino's school that he acquired the interest in reading Roman history which he always retained. Vespasiano, who greatly admired Federigo, included a brief life of him in his collection of the lives of illustrious men. In this life he tells us

---

[39] On Federigo, see James Dennistown, *Memoirs of the Dukes of Urbino,* 3 vols. (London, 1909). This is a new edition with notes by Edward Hutton.

that the Duke of Urbino observed a daily routine of public reading of Livy at mealtime. "When the duke had sat down the doors would be left open, so that all might enter, and he never ate except the hall were full, some one would always read to him; during Lent a spiritual work, and at other times the *Histories* of Livy, all in Latin." [40] Thus, we may see that the same teaching, deriving ultimately from Petrarch, had served as a stimulus for Andrea Bussi, who edited the text of Livy, and for Federigo da Montefeltro, who reflected on the lessons to be derived from studying him. What the scholar elucidated the statesman applied. Nothing could testify more strongly to the strength of the conviction of the importance of historical studies and the relevance of the lessons of history.

When we reach the sixteenth century there is a break and it is signalized by Machiavelli. We know that Machiavelli was exposed during his early years to the traditional admiration for Livy. His father, Bernardo, tells in his *Libri di Ricordi* of the contract with the Florentine book binder for the binding of his copy of Livy and of the payment made by his "figliuolo Niccolo." [41] With this copy Niccolo probably began his intensive reading in Livy, reading that was no doubt suspended during the time when he was employed as secretary of the Florentine chancery, but that was resumed again during his period of enforced leisure and which culminated in the writing

[40] Vespasiano da Bisticci, *Vite di uomini illustri,* L. Frati, ed. (Bologna, 1892), p. 308. English translation by W. G. and E. Waters (London, 1926), p. 108.

[41] Bernardo Machiavelli, *Libro di Ricordi,* C. Olschki, ed. (Florence, 1954), p. 222.

of the *Discorsi* in 1516–1517.[42] We are astonished, however, to find that Machiavelli writes at the beginning of
the *Discorsi* a condemnation of the way in which history
has been taught. He considers that his predecessors have
failed and begins by announcing the originality of his
own approach. "I have decided," says Machiavelli, "to
enter on a path which up to now has been trodden by no
one, and if it brings me labor and difficulty it may bring
me reward . . ." He is astonished and grieved that examples from the history of antiquity are more admired
than imitated. And the more so because in the study of
the civil law or in medicine, "recourse is always had to
those judgments or to those remedies which have been
decreed or provided by the ancients, since the civil law is
nothing else than the opinion of ancient jurisconsults,
which opinions, when they are arranged in order, teach
our present jurisconsults to judge." If the jurisconsults can
be taught to judge according to a body of laws derived
from the history of their profession, why cannot rulers be
taught to rule? Machiavelli declares that he is convinced
that this failure to profit by the example of the ancient
world in the business of ruling men is due "not so much
to the weakness to which the present religion has conducted the world nor to the evils that a proud indolence
has brought on many Christian cities and provinces as to
a lack of a true knowledge of history, through not ex-
tracting the sense of it when reading it and not savoring
the knowledge that it has in itself." [43]

[42] For the date of the *Discorsi,* see Hans Baron, "Machiavelli the
Republican Citizen and the Author of the Prince," *English Historical
Review* 76:217–253 (1961).

[43] Quotations from Machiavelli, *The Prince and the Discourses,* with

Considering the number of appeals to the value of studying history that had been uttered by the humanist educators from the time of Petrarch to that of Machiavelli himself, this indictment appears the more curious. Surely Machiavelli knew that these educators had recommended the study of antiquity for its exemplary character and had pored over it in an effort "to extract the sense of it." The key to Machiavelli's condemnation, however, is to be found not in what the humanists professed but in what they had failed to accomplish. Looking at the political disorder which had come upon Florence, and indeed upon all Italy since the French invasion of 1494, Machiavelli was above all impressed with the contrast between what was preached and what was practiced. He did not condemn a teacher like Vittorino or a ruler like Federigo because they had tried to make the study of history applicable to the present, but because they had not succeeded. The easy confidence of an earlier generation, that it was enough to find out what the lessons of history were and that they would be relevant to the present, was beginning to crack. It is, in this connection, most significant that Machiavelli appeals to the disciplines of jurisprudence and medicine as those which represent the successful use of antiquity.

Machiavelli, whose father was a lawyer, was impressed with the fact that in both medicine and law the particular case was assimilated to a general rule, and this general rule had been tested by many authorities of classical antiquity. Those who had contemplated the course of history had

---

an introduction by Max Lerner (Modern Library, New York, 1940), pp. 104–105.

indeed found examples of virtue and vice, of wisdom and foolishness, but these had never been reduced to a system; there existed no systematic body of knowledge which could be compared to that accumulated by the commentators on the civil law and this was the focal point of Machiavelli's criticism of the humanist tradition—a tradition from which he had himself started, and upon which he had built, but which he found wanting as he reflected on the failure of the Italian political institutions to meet the shock of the northern invasions.

Machiavelli's appeal to the lawyers was founded on a recognition of their prestige and practical success. It is a little like the argument one often hears today that the teachers of law and medicine know what they want and can impart it so that they produce a body of effectively trained students, whereas the teachers of the humanities are vague and inconclusive with the result that their students tend to be a group of ineffectual dilettantes. In the Italian universities of the late Middle Ages and Renaissance the courses on the civil and canon law drew more students than did those on any other subject.

In citing the success of the profession of jurisprudence Machiavelli thus recognized a fact of the current social scene; the same was true to perhaps a less degree of the profession of medicine. Nevertheless his appeal to the lawyers contains an element of paradox. Machiavelli was pleading for both "history" and "system," but the very jurisconsults who most completely realized the ideal of a systematic body of knowledge, applicable to the present, were the least historical.

The greatest figure in the late medieval school of Italian

jurisprudence had been Bartolus of Sassoferrato (1314–1357) whose authority was so great that his opinions were cited by rulers and by courts as if they had the authority of judicial decisions.[44] Bartolus and his followers—the so called post-glossators—were much more interested in the elaboration and application of a system of rules than they were in the achievement of any historical understanding of the growth of law or even of the existence of different periods in the history of institutions. For them the *Corpus* of Justinian was still *de jure* applicable to a Roman empire that had not ceased to exist. It was only necessary to take account of the *de facto* variations which made necessary subtle and elaborate adjustments in the universal rules to fit them to particular contemporary conditions. They did not feel that sense of distance, either from the age of Justinian or from the classical jurists behind Justinian, which we have seen dawning in the thought of Petrarch. In a word their thought may be said to have remained fundamentally medieval in its conception of the relation between antiquity and the contemporary scene.

This school still dominated the teaching of law in the Italian universities in the sixteenth century.[45] Ever since the time of Petrarch, however, its methods and conclusions had been under attack by the humanists. Petrarch's views were forcibly expressed in a letter he wrote in 1340 to a young man from Genoa who had requested advice

[44] On Bartolus, see C. S. N. Woolf, *Bartolus of Sassoferrato* (Cambridge, 1913).

[45] On the law faculties in the Italian universities, see B. Brugi, *Per la storia della giurisprudenza e delle università italiane: Saggi* (Turin, 1915), and *Nuovi Saggi* (Turin, 1921).

about going into the law as a career. Although Petrarch had himself begun by studying the civil law like many others who afterwards became men of letters, he had revolted against it, and he now replied to his young friend with arguments against the lawyers. Petrarch related that he had spent seven years in the study of the law, first at Montpellier and subsequently at Bologna. "If you ask," he wrote, "whether I regret this time today, I say that I do. For I wish to have seen all things so far as it may be permitted to me and I regret and will regret, as long as there is breath in me, so large a part of my life passed by. For I could have done anything else during these years which would have been more noble or more suited to my nature." Recognizing that great glory was formerly sought and achieved by individuals in the study of the civil law, he cites examples from antiquity such as Solon, who, however, as he does not fail to point out, in his old age gave himself to the study of poetry. "The greater part of our legists," he declares, "who care nothing for knowing about the origins of law and about the founders of jurisprudence, and have no other preoccupation than to gain as much as they can from their profession, are content to learn whatever is written in the law about contracts, judgments or wills, and it never occurs to them that the knowledge of arts and of origins and of literature would be of the greatest practical use for their very profession." [46]

The accusations that the lawyers were unhistorical and that they had no interest in the arts were repeated many times by Petrarch's followers. Boccaccio, Salutati, Bruni, Poggio Bracciolini, Maffeo Vegio, and many others joined

[46] Petrarch, *Epistolae,* III, 14–15. My translation.

[30]

in what became a veritable polemic against the lawyers.[47] Among these attacks the most incisive was that delivered against Bartolus by Lorenzo Valla in 1433. In that year the young humanist scholar, already a prodigy who dazzled his contemporaries, had been invited to a chair of rhetoric at the University of Pavia. Like the other Italian universities of this period Pavia contained a faculty of arts and a faculty of law, the latter of which included both civil and canon law. Each faculty had its own organization and its own rector and there had developed considerable rivalry between the two schools. Valla one day encountered a group of law professors who were lavishing uncritical praise on the Bartolists. Someone in the company made the provocative remark that one small treatise by Bartolus, the *De insigniis et armis,* was better than all the works of Cicero put together. Valla made an incredulous reply and then immediately sought out a friend from whom he borrowed a copy of the treatise of Bartolus which he read with a growing sense of indignation and amazement that anyone could have made such a comparison. He then sat down and directed a letter to his friend Sacco who, although on the law faculty, shared Valla's ideas on the value of humanist learning and on correct Latin. In this letter Valla expressed his condemnation of Bartolus's treatise in the strongest language. He began by bewailing the times in which anyone could have preferred a barbarous work of jurisprudence to the golden tongue of Cicero. He pointed out that even in the title of the Bartolist treatise there was an egregious error:

[47] For an account of this literature, see Domenico Maffei, *Gli inizi dell'umanesimo giuridico* (Milan, 1956), especially pp. 33–81.

"insigniis" should have been "insignibus." He described Bartolus as an "ass," "idiot," and "madman," and found his work completely lacking in an understanding of Roman law and institutions. The emperor Justinian, whose work had occasioned so many commentaries, was really to blame and our attention ought rather to be directed to the true sources, to the jurists of the classical period.[48] Valla had originally directed his letter to his friend Sacco, but in order to get wider circulation for his views, he subsequently redirected it to the Milanese humanist, Piero Candido Decembrio. The latter immediately created such hostility among the conservative faction in Pavia that Valla was forced to resign his chair and flee the city.

The humanists continued their attacks on the traditional teaching of the law throughout the fifteenth century and, impatient with the failure of the lawyers to reform, they began themselves to apply to the legal sources techniques of philological and historical criticism. Before the end of the century the great Angelo Poliziano had proposed a critical edition of the famous Florentine manuscript of the *Pandects*.[49] And by the time when Machiavelli was beginning his *Discorsi,* Andrea Alciato was already demonstrating that historical and literary evidence could be applied to the understanding of legal texts. Alciato's first publication was his *Annotationes in tres posteriores Codicis Iustiniani libros* in 1515, which, with the *Annotationes in Pandectas* of Budé published in France seven years earlier, marked the coming of age of the school of humanistic

---

[48] Lorenzo Valla, *Contra Bartolum libellum cui titulus de insigniis et armis epistola* (Basel, 1518). On this work, see Gaeta, *Lorenza Valla,* pp. 195–197, and Maffei, *Gli inizi dell'umanesimo giurdico,* pp. 38–41.
[49] F. Buonamici, *Il Poliziano giureconsulto* (Pisa, 1863).

jurisprudence.[50] Although Alciato himself was never dogmatic or extreme in condemning the Bartolist school and
was willing to recognize the valid achievements of his
predecessors, some of his followers adopted *in toto* the
humanist criticisms and proclaimed that a knowledge of
grammar and philology provided the only sound approach
to the study of the law.

Thus by the second decade of the sixteenth century
there were already two schools of interpretation in legal
studies. The first or traditional school, afterwards known
as the *mos italicus,* emphasized the application to the
present of rules derived from the analysis of the authoritative texts of antiquity. The second, which came to be
known as the *mos gallicus* (because widely adopted by the
French legal scholars), devoted itself to the historical
understanding of the classical law with all the resources
that history and philology could supply, but without
regard to the application of the results to the present.[51]
The aim of the former was systematic, that of the latter
historical. When Machiavelli held up the example of
jurisprudence to those humanists whom he accused of
having failed in their teaching of history, he was in
a sense taking a step backward. The *Discorsi* are in

---

[50] On Alciato, see P. E. Viard, *André Alciat 1492–1550* (Paris, 1926),
and on Budé, Louis Delaruelle, *Guillaume Budé, les origines, les débuts,
les idées maitresses* (Paris, 1907).

[51] On *mos italicus* and *mos gallicus,* see G. Astuti, *Mos italicus et mos
gallicus nei dialogi "de iuris interpretibus" di Alberico Gentili* (Bologna,
1937), and Guido Kisch, *Humanismus und Jurisprudenz: Der Kampf
zwischen mos italicus und mos gallicus an der Universität Basel,* Basler
Studien zur Rechtswissenschaft, vol. 42 (Basel, 1955). See also by Kisch,
vol. 56 in the same series, *Erasmus und die Jurisprudenz seiner Zeit:
Studien zum humanistischen Rechtsdenken* (Basel, 1960).

respect to their attitude toward history nearer Bartolus than they are to Machiavelli's contemporary, Alciato. Although Machiavelli shared with the fifteenth-century humanist tradition the interest in Roman history and the concentration on Livy, he did not believe that examples derived from understanding the text of Livy would produce lessons applicable to the present unless they were systematized. Although he started from the humanist interest in history as it had been initiated by Petrarch, he repudiated the confident humanist assumption that increased admiration and understanding of the text of Livy would automatically be followed by lessons which could be applied to the improvement of the individual and of society in his own time. This assumption, which, as we have seen, had been held in the fifteenth century by such educators as Vittorino and such rulers as Federigo, was perhaps first weakened by the growth, initiated by the humanist scholars themselves, of two schools of interpreting the legal tradition. It was, however, further undermined by Machiavelli's great appeal for the necessity for systematization from historical materials. What had begun in the early Renaissance as a conception of history that combined a real interest in the past with a belief in its relevance to the present was now in the process of being separated into what was to become the "merely historical," on the one hand, and the materials of theoretical structures, political, social, or constitutional, on the other. In the period after Machiavelli the consequences of that separation became clearer in the north than in Italy and the separation is perhaps most dramatically illustrated in France.

Jean Bodin published in 1566 the most philosophical

book on the nature of historical thought written in the sixteenth century. At the beginning of this work he distinguished three kinds of history: divine, natural, and human, which corresponded to three kinds of knowledge: faith, science, and prudence. In the realm of human history, "which flows from the will of men which is ever variable," [52] prudence may be acquired by a comparative study of civilizations with a view to eliciting the general rules of social behavior which may be applied to recurring situations. Like Machiavelli before him he wished to understand the true meaning of ancient history by finding in it examples which had a universal validity. Both of them might be described today as retrospective sociologists. The longest chapter in Bodin's book is devoted to the consideration of the foundations of states and of changes in their constitutions which Bodin considers to be the principal subject matter of history. In this endeavor he finds himself hindered by those who prefer to call themselves grammarians rather than jurisconsults. "We must not look for salvation," he says, in an interesting part of the dedicatory epistle "to those whom no one deigns to consult in matters of law, to those who prefer to consider themselves grammarians rather than jurisconsults, or to those . . . who expect from the power of words alone the safety of the state, the establishment of justice, and the resolution of conflicts. This plague of grammar has in our day so inserted itself into all our disciplines that we have to endure under the name of philosophers, orators, mathematicians and even theologians, petty grammarians who

[52] Jean Bodin, *Methodus ad facilem historiarum cognitionem,* in *Oeuvres Philosophiques de Jean Bodin,* Pierre Mesnard, ed. (Paris, 1951), I, 115. My translation.

are barely out of school. Those who ought to have confined themselves to cleaning lightly the dirt and spots from ancient pictures so as to make the original painting appear, have taken a steel dagger and made such huge and indelible marks on all the books that the image of antiquity can hardly any longer be seen." [53] How we seem to hear the voice of Machiavelli in the indictment of those "who expect from the power of words alone the safety of the state!" But Bodin's repudiation of a part of the humanist tradition goes farther. To condemn the study of grammar for having obscured the image of antiquity was to condemn what had been for the humanists the most important instrument for historical reconstruction. The substance of the complaints against Bartolus of such critics as Petrarch and Valla had been that he did not know language and that this made it impossible for him to understand history. Now Bodin feels that it is the linguistic purists who have destroyed the vision of the past.

Bodin's argument was directed not only against his humanist predecessors but also against his contemporaries. Among them was one whose preeminence as a scholar of the law was unquestioned. Jacques Cujas particularly dedicated his scholarship to the restoration of juridical texts of the pre-Justinian period, and in this he followed faithfully the direction in which Valla's work had pointed. His critical editions and learned commentaries included the discovery and study of interpolations in the text of Justinian's *Corpus* and his principal weapon was precisely that knowledge of grammar, that philology which Bodin had condemned. In the case of Cujas, however, the clearer the image of antiquity became,

[53] *Ibid.*, p. 109.

the less applicable to the modern world did it seem to be, and this was the point of Bodin's criticism. The story is told of Cujas that when his pupils came to him to ask what course they should follow in the terrible crises of the religious struggle, he replied, "Nihil hoc ad edictum praetoris." This has nothing to do with the edict of the praetor.[54] By these words Cujas meant, in the first place, that religious problems ought not to be subject to civil legislation but, secondly and more profoundly, that it was his task to teach history and not to draw from it lessons for the present or the future. The image of antiquity had been recovered but at the same time it ceased to speak directly to the modern world. History was becoming academic. What it discovered might be archeologically true but it was irrelevant to the concerns of a later age. The opposition between Bodin and Cujas would have been incomprehensible to a Petrarch or a Valla. These humanists would not have understood Bodin's condemnation of grammar as a tool of historical understanding or Cujas' lack of interest in the application of the results of historical understanding. For about two hundred years—roughly the period between Petrarch and Erasmus—the humanist tradition, just as it believed in the compatibility of classic and Christian, was able also to combine a deeper historical knowledge of the classical past with an undiminished confidence in the relevance of the lessons of that past. But by the time Cujas gave his response to his students this phase of the Renaissance was over.

[54] Letter of Alexander Scot, "Ad lectorem," prefaced to Jacques Cujas, *Opera omnia* (Lyon, 1606), f⁰ 3r.

INDIVIDUALISM IN
RENAISSANCE HISTORIANS

IN HIS famous work *The Civilization of the Renaissance in Italy,* published in 1860 in Basel, Jacob Burckhardt used an arresting metaphor to describe the difference between Medieval and Renaissance man. "In the middle ages," he wrote, "both sides of human consciousness—that which was turned within as that which was turned without—lay dreaming or half-awake beneath a common veil. The veil was woven of faith, illusion, and childish prepossession, through which the world and history were seen clad in strange hues. Man was conscious of himself only as a member of a race, people, party, family, or corporation—only through some general category. In Italy this veil first melted into air; an *objective* treatment and consideration of the State and of all the things of this world became possible. The *subjective* side at the same time asserted itself with corresponding emphasis; man became a spiritual *individual,* and recognized himself as such." [1]

These sentences serve as introduction to the further analysis of aspects of the development of the individual.

[1] Jacob Burckhardt, *The Civilization of the Renaissance in Italy,* translated by S. G. Middlemore from the fifteenth German edition, introduction by B. Nelson and C. Trinkaus, 2 vols. (New York, 1958), I, 143.

Although Burckhardt regarded the phenomenon which he thus tried to describe as "due above all to the political circumstances of Italy," he found its principal manifestations less in the conduct of affairs of state than in the more nebulous areas of cultural life, and he organizes his description under the three principal topics of personality, glory, and wit. Burckhardt considered that the "free development of personality" included such diverse phenomena as singularity and independence in character, behavior or dress, desire on the part of tyrants to compress the maximum satisfactions into the briefest period of time, emergence in the despotic regimes of the private dilettante, the planning of domestic economy, cosmopolitanism, and, above all, many-sidedness, as illustrated in the careers of such figures as Leon Battista Alberti and Leonardo da Vinci. In defining the importance of the search for fame or glory, Burckhardt cites the fashion for crowning poet-laureates; Petrarch's cult of fame; the tremendous admiration for ancient historians and poets, who by their eloquence had preserved reputations; the collections of lives of famous men; and, among contemporary historians, such as Machiavelli and Giovio, the ascription of "remarkable and dreadful undertakings" to the "burning desire to achieve something great and memorable." Under the topic of ridicule or wit Burckhardt discusses satire as a corrective of too great a preoccupation with fame, as illustrated in the novels of Sacchetti, the role of buffoons and jesters at Renaissance courts, the popularity of parodies, and the mutual attacks of scholars like Poggio and Valla, and he concludes this section on the development of the individual with a consideration of Aretino as the man who most represents these tendencies in individualism.

In spite of the fact that Burckhardt moves from the abstract to the concrete, illustrating his general themes with a particular example, the range of personalities he cites obscures the clarity of his definition. Even if one considers only the greatest figures in Burckhardt's gallery of individuals, Petrarch, Alberti, Leonardo, and Aretino may be "men of the Renaissance," but a combination of their characteristics does not give us a "man of the Renaissance," or a precise definition of individualism. Burckhardt has in fact been attacked by subsequent scholars for applying his term to so wide a variety of phenomena.[2] Does he mean by individualism "the recognition of the individual as an ultimate value," or "moral autonomy," or "the singularity of nature," or "self-assertiveness against authority," or "subjectivity," or some combination of all of these not very precise definitions?[3] Furthermore, were there not in earlier periods notable examples of individualism in such figures as Abelard, St. Francis, and the Emperor Frederick II? Can it be in any sense proven that the individualism of the Renaissance, even supposing agreement on its meaning, was quantitatively more important as well as qualitatively different from previous epochs?

The question of evaluating Burckhardt's concept is still further complicated by the profound changes in the intellectual climate which have occurred in the century since he formulated his ideas on the Renaissance. Burckhardt drew on an intellectual tradition perhaps beginning with

[2] See Wallace Ferguson, *The Renaissance in Historical Thought* (Boston, 1948), *passim,* especially pp. 198 ff.

[3] Cf. Norman Nelson, "Individualism as a Criterion of the Renaissance," *Journal of English and Germanic Philology* 32:316–334 (1933).

Vico, elaborated by Herder and Michelet, and flowering in the historicism of the nineteenth century. This tradition emphasized history as the realm of the unique and the individual and saw positive good in the unfettered realization of the individual's potentiality. In spite of, or perhaps because of the ambiguities of the term, there was sufficient agreement on its connotations so that its values could be celebrated not only in the creative arts but also in the social order. The romantic artist was an individual; so was the entrepreneur who in the pursuit of his own interest was thought to be serving society. Marx's *Das Kapital* had been published only the year before Burckhardt's essay; the economics of Adam Smith still reigned. There was a magnificent confidence in the creativity of the untrammeled individual. In his *Reflections on History,* Burckhardt himself found the highest culture in those periods of history when the collective and authoritarian forces of the state and religion were most reduced in influence.[4] In the middle of the twentieth century, however, in contrast to this positive attitude we often associate individualism with loneliness, insecurity, an anxiety neurosis, and the paralysis of creative powers.[5]

The validity of Burckhardt's conception, thus, has been undermined both by the ambiguities in his definition of individualism and by the changing conceptions of the relation of the individual to society. There are, however,

[4] Jacob Burckhardt, *Weltgeschichtliche Betrachtungen.* The best edition is that of W. Kaegi (Basel, 1941). English translation edited with an introduction by J. H. Nichols (New York, 1943), under the title *Force and Freedom: Reflections on History.* See especially pp. 107–254.
[5] See Erich Fromm, *The Fear of Freedom* (London, 1942), especially pp. 33–117.

certain areas of Renaissance thought and expression which invite further study of the applicability of the Burckhardtian analysis. Of these perhaps the most important is historical writing. Burckhardt himself devoted but little of his discussion of the development of the individual to historical literature. Although he speaks of "the world and history," as "clad in strange hues" in the Middle Ages, with the implication that with the changes of the Renaissance a more objective representation became possible, his citations from contemporary historians are few. He does mention the collections of biographies of the genre *de viris illustribus* and he refers to Machiavelli who in the beginning of his *History of Florence* blamed his humanist predecessors—quite falsely—for not having discussed the effects of political factions in the life of the city. Finally, at the end of the section on glory, he cites the "new" motivation "to achieve something great" which is used as an explanation of the action of individuals in the histories of Machiavelli, Varchi, and Giovio. The historical writing of the Renaissance deserves more, however, than this brief mention in any discussion of the concept of individualism. Renaissance historians were consciously concerned with the individual as political or military leader, as patron of arts and letters, as religious leader. Their pages are filled with analysis of the nature and extent of the influence that could be exercised by one man against the action of fate, fortune, or chance. History provided a wealth of examples for understanding what the great individual could accomplish as well as how far his achievement was circumscribed by factors beyond his control. Discussions of the nature and use of history from Salutati to Machiavelli emphasize its exemplary value and the example is more commonly applied to the course of action of an individual than to an institution or to a social group.[6]

One of the most characteristic discussions of the humanist tradition on historical writing is to be found in a dialogue written by the Neapolitan historian Giovanni Pontano in the last year of the fifteenth century.[7] Although born in Umbria, Pontano had early acquired favor at the Neapolitan court. Alfonso the Magnanimous had entrusted him with responsible offices including the education of his grandson. Under Ferdinand, Pontano became not only official historian but also chancellor and one of the leading figures in the determination of Aragonese policy. He was charged with conducting the negotiations for the treaty of 1486 between Ferdinand and Pope Innocent VIII. With the catastrophe of the French invasion, however, Pontano lost his official position. He tried to gain favor with the French court and so forfeited the confidence of the house of Aragon. Guicciardini later accused him of having shown ingratitude to the dynasty that had so long furnished him with protection and patronage.[8] In these same years he was stricken with a series of private misfortunes the chief of which was the

[6] For Salutati, see his letter to Juan Heredia, *Epistolario di Coluccio Salutati,* F. Novati, ed. (Rome, 1891–1905), II, 289–302. For Machiavelli, *Discorsi sopra la prima deca di Tito Livio,* especially "proemio" in *Opere,* M. Bonfantini, ed. (Milan, 1954), pp. 89–91.

[7] For the events of Pontano's life and the circumstances of the composition of his dialogues, see E. Percopo, *Vita di Giovanni Pontano* (Naples, 1938), pp. 92–106, 221–243. See also *Enciclopedia Italiana* (Milan, 1929–), art. "Pontáno."

[8] Francesco Guicciardini, *La Storia d'Italia,* A. Gherardi, ed., 4 vols. (Florence, 1919), I, 118–119.

loss of his son Lucio. The last period of his life was spent in the shadow of the struggle between France and Spain for the partition of the kingdom of Naples. Like other humanists in times of political misfortune he found consolation in celebrating the claims of the contemplative life and even wrote that his retirement from affairs was a blessing as it enabled him to devote himself unreservedly to literature and philosophy. In these circumstances he reconstructed, partly as history and partly as imagination, the conversations he had enjoyed with his friends in that Neapolitan Academy in which he had long been the leading figure. In the dialogues thus created he was able to express his own views on such subjects as poetry, history, free will, and astrology.

The dialogue *Actius,* which contains the discussions of history and poetry, is named for Pontano's great friend, the poet Sannazzaro, whose political allegiance to the last members of the house of Aragon was more devoted than that of Pontano.[9] The principal interlocutors, who have indeed so much to say that large parts of the dialogue may be described as monologue, are Sannazzaro who speaks on poetry, and another friend of Pontano, Giovanni Altilius, who speaks on history. Both speakers may be taken as representing also the views of Pontano himself.

The *Actius* contains many generalizations which are commonplaces of the humanist tradition on rhetoric. Sannazzaro discourses at length and with a wealth of illustration, especially from Virgil, on the forms of poetry,

[9] The dialogue *Actius* is published in *I Dialogi di Giovanni Pontano,* C. Previtera, ed. (Florence, 1943), pp. 123–239. There is an English translation in Hanna H. Gray, "History and Rhetoric in Quattrocento Humanism" (unpub. diss., Radcliffe College, 1957), appendix.

comparative style, metrics, and other aspects of the subject. When Altilius is begged by his friends to treat history he begins with an analysis of the similarities and differences between history and poetry. This part of the discussion is reminiscent of the distinction made by Aristotle in the *Poetics* between history and poetry. History is what Alcibiades did and suffered; poetry is what any man might do and suffer. According to Altilius history finds facts, poetry imagines them. History is serious and severe while poetry is luxurious and unrestrained. Livy and Sallust are set before the company as the ideal examples for the historian to follow both in thought and expression.[10]

In these general arguments Pontano was not only echoing and developing Aristotelian positions which were characteristic of most of his moral and political writings, but also speaking directly from his own experience. His reputation with his contemporaries had rested chiefly on his Latin poetry, but he had also written a history of the Neapolitan wars which followed the death of his first patron, Alfonso the Magnanimous. The precepts which Pontano puts into the mouths of the interlocutors in the *Actius* are thus not merely traditional but also derived from his own successful achievement in both modes of expression. Among the many points made in the discourse of Altilius on history, there are three statements which may be taken as illustrative of an important part of both the theory and practice of Renaissance historical writing.

The first of these statements is that war must be the principal subject of historical analysis. The historian

[10] *Actius,* pp. 192–194.

should deal with the counsels of those who have recommended resort to war, with the administration of the armed forces, and with the merits of the rival commanders. History deals with *res gestae* and war must be its principal component. A large proportion of the examples chosen from Sallust and Livy are concentrated on the origin and conduct of war.[11]

The second is the proposition that war is especially the realm of the contingent. Nowhere more than in war does the unexpected happen and that which has been hoped for by neither side come to pass. The result is beyond the imagination, beyond the opinions and advice given on each side, beyond hope or fear, beyond rejoicing or sadness. Therefore, the writer must pay great account to chances and fortuitous events in this sphere above all. He must report the weather, hunger, cold, heat, pestilence, and unforeseen dangers in the path of the army as he must also report boldness, fear, treachery, the effect of false rumors, and all that happens in the conduct of war, whether by calculation or by chance.[12]

The third proposition goes beyond either the plans of men or the regular action of nature. The historian must not omit—indeed he has an obligation to report—presages, oracles, prophecies, visions, and sacrifices.[13] These are manifestations to men of the processes behind the appearances of things. Their inclusion in historical narrative was sanctioned not only by current belief but also by the authority of Livy, who never fails to describe the omens

[11] *Actius,* p. 218, lines 4–36.
[12] *Actius,* p. 220, lines 9–17.
[13] *Actius,* p. 218, lines 28–30.

and portents which accompanied a great historical occasion.

The preoccupation with war in this advice to the historian is perhaps natural in Pontano's dialogue in view of the prominence of examples from ancient historical writing, especially Livy and Sallust. It is also natural, however, that Pontano's mind should have seized upon war as the chief subject of history entirely apart from the classical tradition. The memory of the French invasion was fresh. The relative peace of the Italian peninsula had been shattered and a second invasion was overcoming the duchy of Milan even as Pontano was writing. The partition of the kingdom of Naples by the secret Treaty of Granada and the dissolution of the dynasty, in whose service Pontano had spent most of his life, were imminent while he was formulating his rules for the practice of historical writing. The first French invasion, the date of which was to be taken by subsequent historians as marking a new era in the history of European politics, was already beginning to be regarded as a catastrophic break with the past. The analysis of its causes and consequences became one of the great themes of historical writing and it is interesting to juxtapose the precepts of Pontano with the great contemporary histories of the French invasion.

In the year in which Pontano was writing his dialogue a man whom he never had an opportunity to meet, Philippe de Comines, was finishing his *Mémoires,* the last two books of which are devoted to an account of the Italian expedition of the French. Comines was not, at least by any narrow definition, a writer in the humanist tradition. Indeed it may be questioned whether he should be called a Renaissance historian at all. Although Sainte-Beuve and others have not hesitated to describe him as the first of modern writers, they neglect much in Comines that is totally foreign to modern modes of thought. Considering the great differences in the background, education, and experience of Comines and Pontano, it is significant that Comines' account conforms as closely as it does to the criteria set forth by Pontano.

Consider the opening of the seventh book:

. . . to continue these memoirs which I have commenced I intend to describe how it was that Charles VIII now reigning undertook his expedition to Italy . . . There was much disputation whether he should go or not, for the enterprise seemed to all wise and experienced people very unreasonable and those who approved of it were only the king himself and one called Etienne de Vesc, a native of Languedoc, a man of humble birth who had never seen nor understood anything. Another who pushed into this affair, a man of no courage, was a member of the financial administration called Briconnet who has since because of this expedition won great goods in the church as a cardinal and a great many benefices . . . De Vesc had served the king very well in his infancy as a valet and he brought in Briconnet and these two were the cause of the said enterprise which few praised and most blamed because everything necessary to so great an expedition was lacking, for the king was young, weak in his person and full of his own will, unaccompanied by wise counsellors or good leaders. Nor was there any money, for before leaving it was necessary to borrow a hundred thousand francs of the Bank of the Sauli at Genoa reckoned at fourteen per cent interest from fair to fair . . .

They had neither tents nor pavilions and the winter was coming on in Lombardy. One thing they had which may be called good and that was a gay company of young gentlemen full of their own will who did not know the meaning of the word obedience. Thus we must conclude that this expedition was conducted by God from its departure to its return because the wisdom of the leaders counted for nothing. Nevertheless it must be said that they were the cause of bringing great honor and glory to their master.[14]

Throughout his *Mémoires* Comines makes war his principal theme and in this passage, as elsewhere, it can be seen that he gives due weight to the discussion of the counsels that preceded a military undertaking. The plans of men and the course of nature are duly recorded. But most significantly there is also the sense of wonder at the outcome which Comines regards as so far beyond hope or fear that it is the product of direct divine intervention. Not only was the result of the expedition in this sense miraculous, but Comines also recognizes the prophecies and oracles which, according to Pontano, the historian has a duty to report. He records his visit to Savonarola and the things foretold by the friar that had come to pass. Later, at the Battle of Fornovo when the French army is returning to France, Comines considers that again the king has been led directly by God just as Savonarola had foretold.[15]

The appeal to God as conductor of the French expedition has been thought to be ironic and it is certainly true that Comines wished to do all he could to diminish the repute of the immediate advisors of Charles VIII. Nevertheless, throughout the *Mémoires* there is recurring evidence of the seriousness of Comines' sense of the divine rule over human affairs. The rivalry of the European

[14] Philippe de Comines, *Mémoires,* B. de Mandrot, ed., 2 vols. (Paris, 1901), bk. vii, c. 1. My translation.
[15] *Ibid.,* bk. viii, c. 3 and c. 6.

princes is a result of the divine plan which has established
the French against the English, the English against the
Scots, the Spanish against the Portuguese, the common-
wealths in Italy against the despots. The hand of God is
to be seen in prosperity as in adversity. The house of
Spain has had a series of deaths which could have been
predicted by no one and have had a profound effect on
the organization of European politics. Of course, Comines
is not really writing a theodicy, and it may be agreed that
his emphasis is on the kind of prudence which may be
learned by studying the lessons of Louis XI and Charles
the Bold. Yet the area in which lessons of this kind can be
learned at all is circumscribed by acts of God which we
cannot know and Comines' constant recognition of this
fact is often neglected or forgotten. The very critics who
have hailed the modernity of Comines would be the first
to be confounded if modern historians invoked the hand
of God half so much as does Comines.

Some thirty years after Comines had finished his
Mémoires, the greatest historian of the Italian Renaissance,
Francesco Guicciardini, wrote his *Storia d'Italia.* This
history was a product of the last period of his life when
he had seen the failure of all his hopes for the regenera-
tion of politics and society in Italy. As he confessed in his
Ricordi, he had hoped chiefly for three things: the establishment of good government in Florence, the eradication
of the barbarian invaders from the peninsula, and the
reform of the priesthood.[16] In Florence the Medici restoration was leading to the grand duchy of Tuscany, in Italy

---

[16] Francesco Guicciardini, *Ricordi,* in *Opere,* V. de Caprariis, ed.
(Milan, 1953), p. 145.

the Spanish domination was more firmly established than ever, and in the church the beginnings of reform in the Roman curia were hardly perceptible at the time when Guicciardini wrote. There is about his work an atmosphere of resignation. One learns from Tacitus how to conduct oneself under a tyranny. The only way to transcend the historical situation is to try to understand how it has come to be. The opening pages of the *Storia* present the image of the affairs of men as comparable to the sea agitated by winds; the lessons of history will teach us to refer ourselves to the ways of God and not those of men.[17]

Yet within this framework there is a human scheme of causation centered on the analysis of the individual motivations of Ludovico, Alexander VI, Charles VIII, and the other principal actors in the drama of 1494. We have, for example, in direct discourse the speech of Ludovico's ambassadors to the French court about what he *said* were the reasons why he was urging the French king to come to Italy; we have also in Guicciardini's account of the reactions of the French court and the other Italian powers what they *thought* were the motives of Ludovico, and finally we have Guicciardini's analysis of what he was really doing. Thus there is a series of different perspectives, which end by giving us a picture of the impulses and purposes and conditions that had moved the rulers of men. Causation is interpreted as a multiple series of events intersecting at many points. The picture is one of enormous detail and complexity, but it might have been changed by the alteration of a single element in the lives of the characters under consideration.

[17] Guicciardini, *La Storia,* I, 3.

The whole structure of rational analysis is balanced by a recognition of the helplessness of the intellect to penetrate to an ultimate understanding of the processes of history. In the *Ricordi* Guicciardini affirms again and again his belief that we can have no certain knowledge of the future and the contingent. Human affairs are so subject to accident that they cannot be foreseen. One of his arguments for faith is that the things of this world are so unpredictable that help may come to him who has stubbornly persevered when everything has seemed to be against him. This is not an observation on the substance of faith but on its effects. Fortune reigns, but behind the caprices of fortune is a kind of destiny. Neither wise men nor fools can escape that which is to be and they cannot know it in advance. Guicciardini quotes with approval the Senecan maxim that the fates lead those who are willing but drag whose who are not. Miracles are the secret of nature to the depth of which the mind of man cannot penetrate.[18]

In the *Storia d'Italia* the invasion of 1494 is described as accompanied by horrid portents, the account of which vividly recalls how different is the world of the modern historian from that of Guicciardini.

The calamity of Italy was pronounced both by man and by the heavens. Those who profess either by science or by divine inspiration to know the future confessed with one voice that there appeared greater and more frequent mutations, stranger and more horrible portents than had been seen for many years. The rumor resounded throughout Italy that things had been seen beyond the course of nature and the heavens. In Apulia by night three suns were seen in the skies, but clouded in their

[18] Guicciardini, *Ricordi, passim,* especially pp. 102, 110, 122.

centers and accompanied by horrible thunder and lightning. In Arrezzo for many days there passed through the air great numbers of armed men riding on huge horses with a terrible sound of trumpets and tambours. In many places in Italy the images and sacred statues were seen to break into a sweat. Many monsters were born among men and animals and many other things happened in divers parts beyond the order of nature whence the people were filled with an incredible fear.[19]

These brief references to Comines and Guicciardini will serve to indicate how much their exposition follows the precepts announced by Pontano. War is their principal subject matter. They explain the counsels which led to the outbreak of war, the characters and personalities of the military and diplomatic leaders, the strategy and tactics of the armies in the field. They both emphasize how much the course of history lies hidden from human eyes. The outcome is beyond all human calculation of hope or fear. They believe in historical miracles in the sense that something comes to pass quite out of the ken of the men who directed the enterprise, and they also believe in miracles in the conventional sense. They report prophecies and prodigies. Comines relates the prophetic sermons and letters of Savonarola and Guicciardini the monstrous events outside the course of nature that accompanied the entrance of the troops of Charles VIII. Both historians combine a capacity for realistic psychological analysis with a sense of the limits of man's historical understanding. There are determining factors, but they lie outside the course of human history. They are inscrutable.

The question should be raised at this point whether such

[19] Guicciardini, *La Storia*, I, 52–53. My translation.

a system did not paradoxically provide a basis for a more vivid affirmation of human freedom and responsibility than one which locates the determinisms of history within the frame of human or natural action, whence they can be defined and their results at least to some extent predicted. Comines and Guicciardini may be viewed as representing a stage between two different types of historical determinism. The first might be described as a psychological determinism in which the personages of history become types of moral or aesthetic qualities. According to this view, history unrolls from the character of the individual, which is essentially unchangeable. In Sir Thomas More's *History of Richard III,* for example, Richard is born evil in an unnatural manner and remains evil all his life. He is an archetype of villain and tyrant. Another example, from a minor figure who was a contemporary of Comines, is provided by André de la Vigne. He was a court historian of Charles VIII and accompanied the French expedition to Naples, writing a daily chronicle in prose and verse of the king's achievements. For him Charles VIII and his nobles are types of Christian knights engaged in the first preliminaries of a gigantic struggle to free the Holy Land from the invaders. This framework precluded the possibility of the kind of realistic analysis of the character of individuals that we find in Comines and Guicciardini.

The second kind of determinism is that which has become more familiar in the nineteenth and twentieth centuries. It results from the appeal to an inevitable force, sociological, national, or economic, within human history. This is a force the action of which it may be possible to predict, unlike the inscrutable forces of Guicciardini, once it has been distinguished and identified. For example, the great nineteenth-century French historian Michelet, describing the same events with which Comines and Guicciardini dealt, proclaimed that it was inevitable that France had to conquer Italy in this period in order to spread the culture of the Italian Renaissance to the north of Europe. There might have been a Turkish conquest and there might have been a Spanish conquest and either one would have been disastrous had it taken place before the French had had their opportunities in Italy.[20] Michelet is writing the history of the French people, and in the light of the inspired destiny of this great collectivity individual personalities sink into insignificance. Charles VIII and Ludovico Sforza have a dramatic interest, but they do not have an essentially significant part in the story, which would have had the same outcome if some other human puppets had represented the forces that were sweeping the European world. The great motivating power in Michelet's history was the national consciousness of the French people, but the same consequences have followed from economic and psychological explanations that leave the individual subordinated to a remorseless process in which lies the meaning of history.

Such sociological determinisms located within rather than outside human history are, of course, not entirely a creation of the modern mind. Machiavelli has with justification been considered a social scientist, but of all Renaissance historians the one who considered most profoundly the question of the sociological lessons to be learned from

[20] Jules Michelet, *Histoire de France au seizième siècle: La Renaissance* (Paris, 1857), pp. 184–190.

history is Jean Bodin, whose *Methodus ad facilem historiarum cognitionem,* published in 1566, is the most reflective book on history in the sixteenth century.

In the introduction to this work Bodin distinguished divine history, natural history, and human history. Human history is the area controlled by the wills of men forever changing and unlike themselves. Knowledge of this kind of history gives prudence. Natural history discloses the laws of nature and gives men science. Divine history reveals the hand of God in human affairs and gives faith, which is the most certain of all.[21] This analysis may be said to have been the basis of Bodin's life work, for the distinctions he made in this early book became in succession the subjects of each of his major writings—human history in the *République,* natural history in the *Universae naturae theatrum,* and divine history in the *Heptaplomeres,* the strange dialogue on religion which he left unpublished at his death. Of course, these three areas of historical knowledge could not be kept in separate compartments. Bodin saw, as had Comines and Guicciardini, the constant intervention in human affairs of the natural and the divine. Nevertheless, unlike Comines and Guicciardini, Bodin believed, at least at the time when he was writing the *République,* that a kind of certainty could be derived from human history which amounted in certain subjects to the possibility of prediction. The *République* was premised on the proposition that in human history there are valid generalizations that can be made, especially

[21] Jean Bodin, *Methodus ad facilem historiarum cognitionem,* in *Oeuvres philosophiques de Jean Bodin,* Pierre Mesnard, ed. (Paris, 1951), I, 114–115.

on the subject of the rise and fall of states. This is a knowledge about the behavior of men in groups which is far removed from the emphasis of most of Bodin's predecessors with the possible exception of Machiavelli. It was a new direction and there is some evidence that Bodin himself turned away from its full consequences at the end of his life to a more explicit recognition that the course of history is beyond human prediction or control.

In the first edition of the *Universae naturae theatrum* in 1596 Bodin published a letter to a friend in which he praises learning about nature because of its certainty in comparison with the fluctuations of human institutions. He says that even the science of law, which has been called architectonic and the moderator of all the arts, is afflicted with relative standards dependent on the errors and wills of men.

These considerations [he says] drew me back from making an institute of all laws, a selection of which I had made, culled by daily labor from the customs and edicts of almost all peoples so that something fixed might be established. For I believed that all edicts, decrees, and laws of peoples might be boldly attributed to the wills and lusts of men unless there could be discovered in them some shining vestiges of the divine law, that is, a law of nature, guiding a person through the secret places of a labyrinth . . . But in nature there is nothing uncertain. We see that fire burns equally among the Persians as among the Celts and the snow is everywhere white and the orbits of the celestial bodies fixed so that these things which have been decreed remain the same and like themselves from their origin onward. We see that we follow nature as a leader as if it were some divine power . . .[22]

[22] Jean Bodin, Letter to Jacques de Chevrières, prefaced to *Universae naturae theatrum* (Lyons, 1596), p. 3. My translation.

Thus Bodin turned from the uncertainties of the world of man to the certainties of the world of nature, and it is interesting to reflect that one who is rightly regarded as a founder of sociology doubted the basis on which his theoretical structure was built. In the end Bodin's view of history sounds much closer to Guicciardini than to Machiavelli.

In 1954 the Oxford philosopher, Isaiah Berlin, penetratingly discussed the subject of historical inevitability.[23] He found that we have reached a point where we are inhibited from distributing praise and blame or even estimating the importance of an individual and this for two reasons. In the first place, there are those who know too much. These are the followers of a discernible and predictable pattern in history, those who have rejected the idea of historical miracles, who are able to see the unfolding of the historical process without a sense of wonder because everything is explicable. A determinism, economic, sociological, demographic, racial, absolves the individual of responsibility. His behavior is deducible from the laws that govern the larger whole to which he belongs. On the other hand, there are those who know too little to make any judgments. These are the relativists who assert that moral standards must be those of the age to which the individual belongs and there is no more to be said. The behavior of the individual is again deducible from the larger pattern. The result is what Lord Acton condemned in Creighton's account of the Renaissance papacy when he said that Creighton had gone through scenes of raging controversy and passion with divided judgment, a hung jury, and a pair of white gloves.

[23] Isaiah Berlin, *Historical Inevitability* (Oxford, 1954).

INDIVIDUALISM IN HISTORIANS

At least some Renaissance historians were happily free of both of these modern preconceptions. Guicciardini and Comines did believe in the controlling action of fortune or God, but these were interventions which could not be entirely understood or interpreted by the human observer. In effect, they believed in historical miracles. The future was unpredictable, and if the past had in retrospect an air of inevitability to the eye of the observer who was analyzing it, yet this was a product not only of the forces beyond men's ken but also of the wisdoms and follies, the virtues and vices of individuals who made decisions. The historian was free to exhibit on the human plane the cleverness of Louis XI and the foolishness of Charles the Bold, the mistakes of Ludovico Sforza, and the triumphs of Lorenzo de' Medici. The men were more real than the forces because the forces were above the level of human understanding. Nothing is more striking in such writers as Comines and Guicciardini than the sense of reality of the personalities they describe. They are mixtures of good and bad, intelligence and stupidity, not personifications of types. They have dimension and they exist. This means that they had a kind of freedom—perhaps we should say today existential freedom—which involves them in the consequences of their own acts even though they live in a world that comprehends other determinants. They are nearer the characters of tragedy than the modern players in sociological dramas. They are individuals.

The concern of Renaissance historians with describing the actions and reflecting on the moral responsibilities of individuals was no doubt in part a result of their following the historiographic tradition of antiquity. With most of the great ancient historians we have very little to do with what we should call institutions, or social or economic organization or forces. There is a concentration on the analysis of the effects of the thought and action of great men. These men do not live in a world which they can control but the problem how far they can prevail against the fates provides the theme of the most moving pages of history. The confrontation of Scipio and Hannibal has the quality of great drama; their responsibility for their actions is not diminished by being played out against a background of the determination of fate. So it was also with the Renaissance successors of these ancient historians. A view of the importance and the reality of freedom of action of the individual was at the very center of their understanding of the historical world. In the precepts of Pontano, and in the practice of Comines and Guicciardini and their contemporaries, there is abundant justification for the emphasis which Burckhardt put on the concept of individualism in his brilliant picture of their world.

III

THE LAWYERS AND
THE CHURCH IN THE
ITALIAN RENAISSANCE

❧ ❧

I T W A S Edmund Burke who made the remark that a whole nation cannot be indicted and perhaps the same conclusion may be applied to that fraction of a nation which follows a learned profession. It is almost as difficult to describe the legal mind, or the academic mind, as it is that mythical entity—the national character, and it is even more difficult to describe an influence on the rest of society. Nevertheless, a learned profession does consist of a body of men who have had a common education, often have a high *esprit de corps,* and who enjoy to some extent a common social position. Such a group often has an influence extending far beyond its professional function, and it is such a kind of influence which I propose to consider in this study, namely, the relation between the legal profession and the Church in the period of the Italian Renaissance.

It is a truism to say that in every age the history of law has been shaped by the general characteristics of the civilization of which it is a part. The lawyers' attitude toward their profession and their preparation for that profession have been often determined by intellectual interests that far transcend their immediate horizons. Sometimes, however, the process has been reversed and the lawyers have been found in the role of an *avant-garde* creating a significantly new direction in the intellectual life and interests of the community. Such was the case in the Middle Ages when Irnerius and his followers initiated the revival of the study of Roman law at the University of Bologna. In the history of medieval renaissances, the recovery of the text of Justinian's compilation marks one of the most important stages. Indeed, it may be maintained that this legal renaissance, one of the earliest in point of time, was fraught with the most important consequences for the history of European ideas and institutions. Irnerius and his immediate followers were concerned with the establishment of the accurate text of Justinian's *Code* and *Digest*. When this had been accomplished, interest centered on an accurate exposition of the meaning of the text. The method by which this was expounded was that of marginal notes called "glosses." Hence, we call the twelfth and thirteenth centuries the age of the glossators of whom the greatest representative was Accursius who produced his great gloss on the text of Roman law in the twelfth century.

A later generation became more interested in the application of these authoritative texts to contemporary conditions than they were in the further exploration of their historical meaning. This effort to adapt Roman law to feudal and ecclesiastical conditions culminated in the age of the post-glossators in the fourteenth century. Bartolus of Sassoferrato, who produced enormous volumes of commentaries, became recognized as the most significant interpreter. By the time of Bartolus the teaching of civil law was firmly established in many of the Italian and some of the northern universities. A class of notaries, judges, and professors of law had been created whose relations with the cultural life of the community they served have never been sufficiently explored.[1]

In the earliest period of humanism in Italy we find that many of the lawyers contributed directly to the study of classical texts and the enthusiasm for the better apprehension of the classical past. In the pre-Petrarchan circle at Padua, for example, notaries and judges made collections called *florilegia* in which they assembled literary anecdotes and bits of wisdom culled from various ancient authors.[2] In the following period, however, as the interest of humanism became more self conscious, we notice an increasing split between the interests and activities of the lawyers and those of the scholars who followed the *studia humanitatis*.

One of the most characteristic preoccupations of the humanists was their interest in history. Their sense of historical time was largely based upon their researches in philology and their discovery that words could have different meanings in different epochs. Hence was born the notion of anachronism, and anachronism could be used as a weapon of historical criticism. This destroyed the basis of the Bartolist position, and the humanist invective against the lawyers became more intense; it fol-

[1] On Bartolus, see C. S. N. Woolf, *Bartolus of Sassoferrato* (Cambridge, Eng., 1913).
[2] See Roberto Weiss, *The Dawn of Humanism in Italy* (London, 1947), *passim,* and Beryl Smalley, *English Friars and Antiquity in the Early Fourteenth Century* (Oxford, 1960), conclusion.

lowed very much the pattern of the critique already directed against the scholastic philosophers. We find Maffeo Vegio, for example, in the second quarter of the fifteenth century condemning the lawyers for their lack of history and even blaming the compilers of Justinian's *Digest* for having proceeded in an unhistorical manner.[3] Lorenzo Valla in 1433 delivered the bitter attack on Bartolus which cost him his chair of rhetoric at the University of Pavia.[4]

Valla's attack on the medieval jurists marked perhaps the high point of the humanist criticism of the Bartolist tradition. This criticism, however, continued in a whole series of treatises for the remainder of the fifteenth century and the repetition of satiric judgments directed against Bartolus and his followers became a commonplace of humanist discourse.[5] In spite of this criticism, however, the prestige of the professional teachers of law in the legal faculties of universities continued to grow. In fact the courses given by the great professors of law became more popular than ever. Students flocked from all parts of Italy and from the north to the great universities where a tradition of legal instruction had existed from the beginning. At Bologna, at Padua, at Pavia, at the University of Pisa, reconstituted after 1472, the lawyers enjoyed the greatest position and had by far the largest number of followers. In the official rolls of the University of Pisa in

[3] Maffeo Vegio, "Proemio" to *De Verborum Significatione,* in G. A. Sassi, *Historia literaro-typographica mediolanensis* (Milan, 1745), col. ccccvii.

[4] See the discussion earlier on pp. 31–32.

[5] For an excellent survey of this literature, see Domenico Maffei, *Gli inizi dell'umanesimo giuridico* (Milan, 1956), pp. 33–78.

the period from 1472 to 1525 we find that 101 appointments were made in civil law, and 71 in canon law, whereas there were but 13 in theology. Of course, it must be recognized that students did not come to Pisa primarily for theological studies and there was provision in Florence for instruction in philosophy and theology. Nevertheless, the number of appointments in the Pisa law faculties, the controversies that arose over the candidates, and the high salaries the lawyers demanded and received all testify to the prestige of the profession.[6]

The effort to secure the services of the most eminent professors of civil and canon law became even more tense than it had been in the preceding period. We find the Republic of Florence intervening, for example, to prevent Bartolommeo Sozzini from leaving the University of Pisa to accept an appointment at Padua under the authority of Venice.[7] This episode was followed by appeals from Siena to the papacy on behalf of Sozzini and admonitions from the pope to the government of Lorenzo de' Medici.

Another celebrated legal figure who became an object of contention in the early sixteenth century was Filippo Decio, for whose services there was competition not only between the Italian powers but also between the King of France and the Republic of Venice. Decio assumed a tone

[6] For the appointments to the faculties at Pisa, see Angelo Fabroni, *Historiae academiae Pisanae,* 3 vols. (Pisa, 1791), I, 379–400. For the discussions of candidates and salaries, see the documents on the University in the Archivio di Stato in Florence, especially "Deliberazioni degli ufficiali dello studio, reg. 419," and "Lettere dello studio, reg. 427."

[7] On the detention of Sozzini by the Florentine government, see Angelo Fabroni, *Laurenti magnifici vita,* 2 vols. (Pisa, 1784), II, 78–80. See also G. Tiraboschi, *Storia della letteratura italiana,* 16 vols. (Milan, 1824), vol. VI, pt. 2, pp. 829–838.

of arrogance in dealing with the Florentines, the Venetians, and the French which was justified by his conviction
that he could name his own terms. Louis XII was even
willing to risk a diplomatic incident with Venice in order
to persuade Decio to accept a position at the University
of Pavia.[8]

Such luminaries of the scholarly legal profession as
Decio, Alciato, and Sozzini were furthermore recipients
of salaries altogether out of proportion to what was earned
in any other area of academic life. The salary offered Decio
by the Florentines in 1515 rose to the unheard-of figure of
1000 florins annually in order to retain the services of this
distinguished professor against invitations from Venice
and Milan.[9] Many such negotiations were conducted in an
atmosphere singularly like that which surrounds the attempts today to "raid" rival universities to acquire a name
that will bring additional prestige to a faculty. In addition
to the larger financial rewards all kinds of privileges were
often stipulated in these sixteenth-century contracts between the governing officials of a university and the new
incumbent. Such prvileges included special concessions
for favorable hours of lecturing, establishment of areas of
subject matter on which rival professors could not in-
trude, and grants of special precedence in academic ceremonies.[10] Frequently the result of concessions like these

[8] Tiraboschi, vol. VI, pt. 2, p. 864. See also the extremely interesting
life of Decio by his pupil Boeza, published as a preface to *Decii commentarii in Digestum vetus* (Venice, 1589). This contains copies of
many of Decio's letters.

[9] Contract of 27 April 1515 in Florence, Archivio di Stato, reg.
ufficiali dello studio, fol. 496.

[10] *Ibid.*

was to swell further the arrogance and intransigence of the recipients so that the small class of highly successful professional lawyers developed a style characterized by insufferable arrogance and pomposity and constant bickering with each other and with their employers. It is not surprising that they became the object of the bitter satiric attacks of Rabelais and others in the sixteenth century.

The prestige which these professors were able to claim and often to attain was built in part on the fact that a legal education was a practical necessity for anyone who aspired to have a career in the affairs of Church or State, whether or not he hoped to become a practicing lawyer. When Giovanni de' Medici, the son of Lorenzo the Magnificent, had been made a cardinal at the age of fourteen, his father was advised to cease any further education in classical Latin and put him to the study of the law which would be of the greatest value to him in his future high situation. He was accordingly enrolled among the pupils of Decio at the University of Pisa.[11] Likewise among Decio's pupils either at Pisa or at Florence had been Cesare Borgia and Francesco Guicciardini.[12] Many of the great figures of literature from Petrarch to Montaigne had studied the law even though they afterwards revolted against it, and we should not forget that Luther at least began the study of the law before his conversion and that Calvin spent years studying the Roman law under the best masters of France and Italy. Under these conditions the methods, the attitudes, and the incidental opinions

[11] G. B. Picotti, *La giovinezza di Leone X* (Milan, 1927), p. 236.
[12] For Borgia, see Charles Yriarte, *Caesar Borgia,* translated by William Stirling (London, 1947), p. 30. For Guicciardini, see R. Ridolfi, *Vita di Francesco Guicciardini* (Rome, 1960), pp. 12–14.

of the law professors take on an importance far transcending their technical instruction. In many ways they contributed to forming the mind and style of their age.

Even rulers and governments condescended on particular occasions to take an interest in the harangues and lectures of the jurists. Lorenzo de' Medici himself, accompanied by his friend Angelo Poliziano, came to the University of Pisa to hear a debate between the Milanese lawyer Giasone (or Jason) del Maino and the Sienese professor Bartolommeo Sozzini on an occasion when both had been teaching at the University and Sozzini had challenged del Maino on his ability to interpret texts of the Roman law. This debate created an intense interest among the audience and so keen was the competition between these two eminent scholars that each of them was afterwards accused of having forged texts of the *Digest* in order to win his case. The very fact that the charge could be made indicates how much stock was put in the victory in such a contest.[13] At a later date, in the period when the French were occupying the Duchy of Milan, King Louis XII with his court came to the University of Pavia to hear del Maino expound a text of the *Digest*.[14] These incidents are sufficient to indicate the high esteem in which the legal profession was held and the degree of influence that could be exerted by the most eminent

---

[13] There is an account of the debate in Allegreto Allegretti, *Diari,* published in *Rerum Italicarum Scriptores,* L. A. Muratori, ed., 25 vols. (Milan, 1723–1751), vol. XXIII, cols. 768–860. The story of the forged texts is in Panzirolus, *De claris legibus interpretibus* (Leipzig, 1721), art. "Sozzini."

[14] The visit of Louis XII to the lecture of Jason del Maino took place in 1507. Cf. F. Gabotto, *Giasone del Maino e gli scandali universitari nel quattrocento* (Turin, 1888), p. 237.

professors of civil law. It is hardly possible that these men who taught thousands of students, many of whom were bound for other than conventional legal careers, should not have influenced their students' thinking even on subjects not directly related to the texts of the Roman law. One of the most interesting questions which may be asked about this influence concerns their relation to the Church and the ideas that they may have imparted to their pupils about the ecclesiastical establishment.

In discussing the attitude of the legal scholars toward the Church examples will be selected from the period roughly between 1490 and 1520 and from among the men whose reputations with their contemporaries was highest.

Jason del Maino was perhaps the most prominent figure among professors of law in the latter part of the fifteenth century.[15] He was born in 1435 at Pesaro where his family was living in exile from Milan because they had taken part in a conspiracy against the ruling Visconti. He considered, however, that Milan was his *patria* because it had been his father's home and, as the family were connected with the Sforza, they came to occupy a prominent position in the duchy after the change of dynasty in 1450. Jason entered the University of Pavia in 1454 where he embarked upon the study of law. One of his masters was the same Catone Sacco to whom Valla had written his letter attacking Bartolus and the medieval jurists. Thus, in Jason's education we find mingled elements of the humanist tradition and the medieval jurisprudence.

[15] For Jason's biography see the work by Gabotto and the *Enciclopedia Italiana* (Milan, 1929–), art. "Giasone del Maino."

HUMANISTS AND JURISTS

At first Jason seemed to take but little advantage of his opportunities. He wasted his time in riotous living and a series of student escapades. Finally, his father agreed to pay his debts and Jason apparently entered upon a reformed career and gave himself to serious study, learning classical languages as well as the law. Of Latin authors Sallust became his favorite and quotations from Sallust appear frequently in his later works. In 1461 he moved to Bologna, the oldest and at that time the most celebrated of legal faculties, in order to study with Alexander Tartagna of Imola and with Francesco Accolti who were the most respectable representatives of the Bartolist tradition. Returning to Pavia he took his doctorate in civil law in 1467. This was immediately followed by his nomination as professor at Pavia, a nomination undoubtedly influenced by the connections his family enjoyed with the Sforza.

From the beginning Jason's lectures were extraordinarily successful. He commenced his course with commentaries on the *Code* and continued by taking up the first book of the *Digest*. His first publication was a treatise on tenures in 1477 and this was followed by extensive volumes of commentaries on the *Digestum Vetus*, on the *Infortiatum*, and on the *Digestum Novum*. In 1485, after his reputation had been brilliantly established, he was called to the University of Padua and the service of Venice, and there he remained for three years and then removed to Pisa, the university which had recently been reconstituted by Lorenzo de' Medici. His career at Pisa was exceptionally stormy, involving prolonged controversy with Filippo Decio, who had formerly been his pupil, and with Bartolommeo Sozzini, the irascible jurist of Siena. Under these circumstances his professorship at Pisa was soon terminated and he returned to Pavia where he taught for most of the remainder of his life during the period of the French occupation as well as during the last days of the Sforza dynasty. He died in 1519 full of honors and in possession of a considerable fortune. He had been made councillor and senator by Ludovico il Moro and by virtue of his connection with the Sforza family he assumed the title of count and knight. He served the state of Milan as ambassador on the occasion of the election of Alexander VI to the papacy and he was given many titles and rewards by Louis XII, who honored him on one occasion, as noted above, by coming in person with members of his court to hear Jason expound a text of the *Digest*. His motto was, appropriately enough, "Fortune comes to him who deserves it."

In his will he provided for numerous charitable bequests and also made regulations for the erection of his tomb with the curious inscription, "Here lies Jason del Maino, whoever he was" [*quisquis ille fuit.*] This epitaph is still to be seen in the Church of St. Anthony in Pavia. Another and much more elaborate epitaph was circulated and is recorded in contemporary eulogies of Jason, but was never inscribed on a monument. This epitaph in Latin verses consists in a curious dialogue of which the following is a free translation: "Who lies in this tomb?" "Who?" "The great Jason." "Do you mean him who was enriched by the golden fleece?" "One far more famous than that Jason." "Who then, I beg of you?" "Jason del Maino, the great glory of the Imperial law. There was no one more learned in the law than he, nor anyone who could better restore the dead law of the ancients." [16]

In his attitude toward the ecclesiastical establishment and toward the doctrines of the Church Jason appears to have been a comfortable conformist. There was even published at one time a rumor that he aspired to be named a cardinal by Pope Julius II. His lectures opened with the appropriate invocations, and in his writings and in his will we find the formulas of the conventional religious appeals. Furthermore, he participated fully in such contemporary observances as pilgrimages and the glorification of relics. On one occasion he asked the Venetian government to grant him a safe conduct in order that he might make a visit to the bones of St. Anthony at Padua.[17]

With all this there are, nevertheless, indications that Jason's interests were only conventionally directed toward the observances of religious beliefs. Certainly in the period of the intense struggle between Louis XII and Julius II at the time of the Council of Pisa in 1511 Jason preserved a neutrality which made it possible for him to continue his career without opposition from either king or pope. Most interesting in this connection is an exhortation which Jason gave to his students at the opening of his course in Padua in 1487. This exhortation is printed at the beginning of his commentaries on the first part of the *Digest*. It consists almost entirely of a paraphrase of Sallust's first paragraph in his history of Catiline's conspiracy.

[16] Both epitaphs are printed in B. Rutilio, *Iurisconsultorum Vitae* (Basel, 1537), pp. 234 ff.

[17] For the offer of the cardinalate, cf. Gabotto, *Giasone del Maino*, p. 239, and for the visit to Padua, *ibid.*, p. 271.

Jason pointed out to his students that humankind was divided into body and soul, that the body was mortal while the soul was immortal, and that it was necessary, therefore, to cultivate those virtues which partake of the soul rather than those pursuits which are served by the body. He closed by quoting Isocrates who had said to the King of Cyprus, "Since your body is mortal and your soul immortal, strive that by the benefits of your virtues you may have an immortal memory of your soul." [18] It is the immortality of the memory of the soul in this world for which Jason is pleading, that is to say, fame rather than immortality in a conventionally Christian sense. Indeed, although Jason had changed a few words in Sallust's paragraph in order to make the language more palatable to Christian ears, there is very little in the passage that would not be found perfectly acceptable in a world which had not known Christianity. To argue from this one exhortation to his students that Jason was less Christian than many of his contemporaries would doubtless be to go too far. We can, however, see in this passage how much the familiar theme of fame and interest in the survival of one's reputation had gripped him and, to this extent, he represents both medieval and renaissance traditions. A far more apparent revolt against the Church can, however, be traced in his celebrated pupils.

Among these was Filippo Decio, the younger son of a family of the minor nobility in Milan during the period of the Sforza rule.[19] Educated originally in literature

---

[18] Jason del Maino, *Commentarii in digestum vetus,* 4 vols. (Lyons, 1547), vol. I, preface. My translation.
[19] See the life of Decio by his pupil Boeza, printed as preface to *Repertorium in Commentaria* (Lyons, 1550). See also the essay by

and the arts to serve the Sforza as a humanist secretary, Decio was attracted to the profession of the law by the example of his elder brother. He attended the University of Pavia and had so successful a career there that he acquired a reputation as a prodigy and began at a very young age to hold public disputations, which gained for him the admiration of both students and faculty. In 1473 he was called to the University of Pisa, at first, in a minor capacity, but his talents soon won him an appointment from Lorenzo de' Medici to a regular position in the academic hierarchy. Decio then entered upon a stormy career in the university marked by rivalries and dissensions not only with other professors but also with the officials of the university in Florence. He complained of his salary, of the hours in which he had to lecture, and of the degree of prestige which was accorded him. In spite of these difficulties his salary was regularly advanced until he was receiving more than any other professor. After the French invasion of 1494 the university entered upon a difficult period and Decio was willing to listen to invitations from elsewhere. He accepted a post at Padua in the service of the Venetians in 1501 but left abruptly four years later on the urgent request of King Louis XII himself to return to the University of Pavia. When the French king entered into his conflict with the pope in 1510, the legal advice of Decio was solicited to support the French dominated Council of Pisa, and Decio was willing to argue for the king that the legal power to convoke an ecumenical council resided not only in the

F. Gabotto, "Un Giureconsulto del quattrocento," in *Conversazione della domenica* (Milan, 1887), and *Enciclopedeia Italiana,* art. "Decio."

college of cardinals as a whole but also in a part thereof or even, in certain circumstances, in the cardinals as individuals. Decio's advice to the king of France on this occasion was afterwards published in a *consilium*[20] which is of interest in indicating the position that an eminent lawyer of professed orthodoxy could take toward the papacy on the eve of the Reformation.

Decio opens his argument by protesting that the matter is of great weight and seriousness and that he runs the risk of being thought to attack the supreme pontiff to whose predecessor he owed his appointment as auditor of the Roman Rota. Nevertheless he is determined to speak out for the truth. He affirms that he proposes to treat the question *de jure* and not the contemporary condition of fact.

He considers that the problem involves four principal questions which must be answered if a true solution is to be found. These questions are:

1. Whether the pope can be accused if he is so incorrigible in crime that the Christian religion suffers a scandal.
2. Whether a pope is so bound by his own solemn engagements that he cannot free himself from them.
3. Whether in the above and similar cases a general council can make a judgment against a pope.
4. What should be the manner and form of celebrating such a council.

In discussing the first question Decio first marshals all the arguments from the canon law and from the commentators which seem to support the proposition that the

---

[20] F. Decio, *Consilia sive responsa,* 2 vols. (Frankfort, 1588), consilium CLI, pp. 163–169. This *consilium* was frequently suppressed or cancelled in editions of Decio's collected works.

pope cannot be judged by any human authority. He then declares, however, that, notwithstanding these precedents and opinions, he believes the contrary to be the law. He cites certain cases in which he considers that all the doctors are agreed that the pope can be judged. These include heresy, a pope's voluntary subjection to a council, a pope's confession to his confessor, and the case of schism in which there are two contenders for the papacy. There is also a fifth case, namely, that in which the pope is in notorious delict to the scandal of the Church. Although Decio admits that there is more disagreement on this case, he himself is convinced that the same rules of law apply as to the previous cases, and therefore concludes that a pope who has so scandalized the Church can be judged.

His argument and conclusions on the remaining three questions follow the same pattern. After examining the authorities on both sides of the question, Decio concludes that a pope cannot free himself from solemn engagements into which he has earlier entered, that a general council can judge a pope, and that it pertains to the college of cardinals or even to a part of that body to summon a council to act against a pope who has fallen into manifest delinquency. These conclusions were, of course, the product of Decio's employment by the King of France to argue against Julius II. They were nevertheless supported by a wealth of citations and the high professional competence of their author. Very little of Decio's argument was original; for the most part it depended on theories developed in the time of Marsilius of Padua and William of Occam and elaborated during the conciliar period. Nevertheless, his *consilium* contains some ingenious reasoning, especially on the *ius colegii* and the right of a part of the college of cardinals or even a single member to represent the whole body. Even though the position of Decio was dictated by self-interest and the rewards he expected from King Louis XII, it is significant that a respectable academic argument could be levelled against the jurisdictional claims of the papacy by a high professional authority.

Decio's treatise was answered on behalf of the papacy by one Angelo Leonora, a Vallombrosian monk, who composed an apologia *pro Papa Julio*.[21] Leonora was a man greatly inferior in ability to his opponent and his treatise in defense of the orthodox position is of little interest. Julius II was, however, not content to limit himself to commissioning a reply to Decio's *consilium* and proceeded to take more violent measures against the lawyer who had dared to oppose him and to give a color of justification to the proceedings at Pisa. The tone of the exchange between the *papa terribile* and the arrogant professor is characteristic of both.

Even before the pope had heard that Decio had decided to support the French interest at Pisa he wrote a brief, dated 27 August 1510, to Decio charging him with illegal use of the title of Auditor of the Roman Rota and threatening him with excommunication if he did not abandon it at once.[22] Decio wrote an arrogant reply and

<hr />

[21] Angelo Leonora, *Apologeticum Angeli ananchorite Vallisumbrose pro Julio Papa contra concilium Decii* (1511).

[22] For the text of this brief as well as the other correspondence between Decio and Julius II, see the copies printed in Boeza's life of Decio, cited in note 19.

recommended to His Holiness that he reprimand those who persuaded him to write such a letter.

When Julius II began to prevail over the Council of Pisa Decio tried to dissociate himself from further proceedings with the schismatic cardinals. It was, however, too late and Decio was excommunicated with the offending cardinals. Decio eventually fled to France and thence wrote a letter to the pope begging to be granted a pardon. On 9 September 1512 when all was going well for the causes supported by the pope in Italy, Julius wrote to Decio and another lawyer who had supported the council and desired them to come to Rome to explain the grounds they had found for their arguments against the papacy, promising a safe-conduct if they did so. This offer Decio perhaps wisely refused, but he wrote to the Cardinal del Monte giving an account of his adventures and explaining that he had been required by royal majesty to write in behalf of the council. In this letter he announces that he had also appealed to the Cardinal de' Medici because the latter had been his pupil at the University of Pisa. He begs the cardinal to arrange with His Holiness that he be absolved of all censures.

In spite of these disavowals of his support of the council Decio continued in France, at the request of the remaining Pisan group, to give *responsa* and to furnish arguments against the defenders of the papacy. With the accession of Leo X, however, it became easier to arrange an accommodation: by a brief of October 23, 1515, Decio was absolved and appointed to the professorship of canon law in Rome. By this maneuver the papacy was able to silence any further expression of opinion from its hostile and authoritative critic. Nevertheless, Decio's *consilium* remained in print and, although frequently censored in subsequent editions of his work, it became a standard source during the Reformation debates for legal arguments against the papacy. The probability that Decio had acted largely from personal and mercenary motives could not obscure the fact that one of the most eminent and respected professors of civil and canon law, whose orthodoxy in matters of doctrine was unquestioned, had undermined the legal basis of the *plenitudo potestatis* of the papacy.

A still more daring attack on the institutions of the contemporary Church came from the pen of Andrea Alciato, who was universally regarded as the leading jurisconsult of his generation. Likewise a pupil of del Maino, Alciato was a Milanese educated at Pavia but his influence extended far beyond that of his masters. He taught in France in the universities of Avignon and Bourges as well as in the great Italian centers. He became the friend and correspondent of Erasmus and many other humanists of his generation and combined to a previously unprecedented degree a knowledge of classical literature, history, and sources of Roman law. Indeed he became the founder of a new school of jurisprudence, based on the principles of humanist exegesis with an appreciation of the importance of the interpretation of the Roman law as a living common law as it had been developed by Bartolus and other practitioners of his school. He lived through the first half of the sixteenth century and although in the end he remained loyal to Rome, some of the works of his early career, particularly in the period before Luther made his protest, show how tenuous was his acceptance of the orthodoxy into which he had been born.[23]

Among these works is a little treatise *Contra vitam monasticam* written probably in 1515 or 1516.[24] This is in the form of a letter to a friend who Alciato has heard has entered a monastic order. This step has so distressed Alciato that he marshals all the arguments he can think of against the institution of monasticism in an effort to dissuade his young friend from this decision. He attacks the issue on its most fundamental basis by examining not only the abuses but the very *raison d'être* of the monastic vows. Although the times he feels are such as to prevent him from being entirely frank, he is willing to maintain that the life of Christians who live in the world as Christians but free from sacred vows is more acceptable to God than a separate order set apart from the world and presumed to accumulate a special merit in heaven. This is the original and striking note in Alciato's argument; he raises a question which was to find an answer in the revolutionary rejection of monasticism by so many of the leading figures in his own and the immediately succeeding generation. An institution that had lasted more than a thousand years in Western Christendom crumbled in the sixteenth century. Erasmus, Luther, Rabelais, and many lesser figures repudiated a conventual existence and in different ways proclaimed that the true Christian

[23] On Alciato, see P. E. Viard, *André Alciat, 1492–1550* (Paris, 1926). See also G. Barni, *Le Lettere di Andrea Alciato* (Florence, 1953), with the corrections supplied by R. Abbondanza in "A Proposito dell'epistolario dell'Alciato" *Annali di storia del diritto* 1:467–500 (1957).

[24] The *Contra vitam monasticam* is printed in Barni, pp. 265–289.

life could be realized in the world. The letter of Alciato shows that this revolution was by no means limited to those who had experienced the monastic discipline.

The less original line of argumentation in the letter contrasts the early history of monasticism with its present manifestations. Alciato denies that monasticism was an institution of the primitive Church, but, nevertheless, even after it was established it existed in a purity that has sadly degenerated in recent times. Although monks in the early days were ready to suffer martyrdom for the faith, the monks of today shrink from any sacrifice, even when much of Christian Europe is oppressed by the alien Turk. Monasticism in the time of St. Francis was devoted to the poor and St. Francis himself lived by this rule. If he could return to life now what would he think of the Franciscan order? Turning to a different line of argument and one which was to be echoed in the eighteenth century by Gibbon, Alciato voices the opinion that perhaps the Roman empire fell because there were too many monks, and men were deflected from patriotic and military service. He maintains that it requires no courage to embrace the monastic life and concludes that on every ground, historical, moral, or dogmatic there is no justification for the step his friend has taken.

Alciato confided his treatise to a scholarly friend of his, who was a bookseller in Bologna. This friend in turn sent the manuscript to Erasmus who he rightly thought would be interested in it because of the strictures on monasticism in the *Praise of Folly* which was then circulating in the European world. After the condemnation of Luther Alciato began to fear for his own reputation and he wrote to Erasmus to see whether he could recover the manuscript of this work on so dangerous a subject.[25] Erasmus replied saying that Alciato's work was in safe hands and that he need fear nothing but he did not return the manuscript.[26] Later appeals met with a similar fate and Erasmus, in fact, never returned the treatise nor did he destroy it as Alciato had begged him to do. On Erasmus's death it passed with his other manuscripts to his heir, Boniface Amerbach of Basel, and from him it eventually found its way to the Netherlands where it was published in the seventeenth century and immediately put on the Index by the Roman Church.[27] Alciato's deviations from orthodoxy were thus known to but few in his lifetime and the most respected lawyer of his generation was able officially to dissociate himself from Protestantism.

It is obviously impossible to suggest conclusive generalizations from the few examples considered here. It is, nevertheless, a significant fact that two lawyers as eminent and influential as Decio and Alciato should have attacked such fundamental parts of the ecclesiastical structure as the position of the papacy and the institution of monasticism. The *consilium* of Decio was public, while the treatise of Alciato was privately circulated, but we cannot help wondering whether the thousands of students who heard these men lecture imbibed similar views or at least hints of antagonism toward the contemporary Church. In any age gifted lecturers give to their students

[25] P. S. Allen, ed., *Opus epistolarum Des. Erasmi Roterodami,* 12 vols. (Oxford, 1906–1958), IV, no. 1250.

[26] *Ibid.*

[27] G. Barni, "Alciato giureconsulto Milanese e le idee della Reforma Protestanta," *Rivista di storia di diritto Italiano* 21:161–209 (1948).

far more than a mass of professional information and in
the view of the world presented by the great lawyers of the
Renaissance we should not be surprised to find a considerable strain of anticlericalism, manifest in many
different ways. It appears not only in formal treatises on
points of institutions and dogma but also in hundreds
of *consilia* and records of particular cases. Lawyers who
entertained doubts on the validity of monasticism were
apt to deal severely with monasteries in cases involving
property rights. Even lawyers who taught courses in canon
law as Decio did could whittle away the rights of clerics
when these were invoked in particular cases. The many
tomes of *consilia,* case books, commentaries, and treatises
on special subjects need to be searched to investigate
further the attitude of the lawyers toward the ecclesiastical establishment.

On the basis of the indications before us a few tentative
generalizations on this subject may be suggested.

In the first place it is clear that the lawyers not only
reflected but also positively contributed to the growth of
a secular attitude in fifteenth- and sixteenth-century Italy.
When Guicciardini, for example, states his low opinion
of the Church,[28] which he nevertheless served so well,
may we not trace one element in that attitude to what he
had learned in the study of the law under Filippo Decio?

Secondly, among the lawyers the long discussion in the
fifteenth century of the correct method of studying the
law led at least some to be more receptive initially to the
reformers. After all, the latter proposed to teach the Chris-

[28] Francesco Guicciardini, in *Opere,* R. Palmarocchi, ed. (Milan,
1942), II, 753.

tian texts in the same way in which the lawyers were
expounding the *corpus iuris*. A difficult passage in St.
Paul was to be understood by the application of the same
techniques of historical and philological explanation as
had been applied to a difficult text in Justinian's *Digest*.
Was not the attack on Trebonian by the humanist lawyers
parallel to the attack on the scholastic theologians by the
followers of the new learning? Not only in Italy but also
in the rest of Europe the early years of the Reform show
a significant number of adherents to the new doctrines
recruited from the legal profession. The Piedmontese
lawyer Giovanni Nevizzano published in 1518 the first
edition of his influential *Silva Nuptialis*.[29] This treatise
contained an analysis of the arguments for and against
the institution of marriage and a discussion of the conflicts in the civil and canon law governing marriage
contracts and impediments to concluding them. The
author used his opportunity to include many digressions
and to display his knowledge of ancient literature. Questions of political theory, the authority of princes and
bishops, and the settlement of differences between Guelfs
and Ghibellines were all said to be derived from the
consideration of marriage. In the edition of 1522 and in
subsequent editions Nevizzano quoted frequently with

[29] On Nevizzano and the *Silva Nuptialis*, see C. Lessano, *La Sylva
Nuptialis di Giovanni Nevizzano* (Turin, 1886). The complete title of
the treatise reads: *Silvae Nuptialis Libri VI in quibus ex dictis moder-
norum materia matrimonii, dotium, filiationis, adulterii originis, suces-
sionis, et monitorialium plurissime discutitur. Una cum remediis ad
sedendum factiones Guelphorum et Ghibellinorum. Otem modus indi-
candi et exequendi iussa Principum. Ad haec de autoritatibus Doctorum
privilegiisque miserabilium personarum. Quae omnia ex questione An
nubendum sit vel non desumpta sunt.*

approval from the sermons and other writings of Martin Luther. Although the work was dedicated to a bishop, it is filled with denunciations of the ambition and greed of ecclesiastics and the corruption from which the Church is said to be suffering. Nevizzano was one of the earliest voices in Italy to welcome Luther's call to reform and his work was later put on the Index.

Among those who subsequently took up the cause of the Reform were the distinguished lawyer, Matteo Gribaldi Mofa, and the members of the Sozzini family who represented one of the great dynasties of legal scholars in Italy and who now gave to the world the heresy identified by their name.[30] In the north the constellation of legal names initially attracted to the Reformation is even more striking. In France it includes the great legist Dumoulin, the great humanist student of the law Budé, and among later figures, Connan, Duaren, Hotman, and Bodin. In Germany and Switzerland Zasius and Amerbach received the first manifestations of the Reformation as the dawn of a new age. Nor must it be forgotten that the legal training of Calvin in a school of interpretation founded by Alciato was an important part of his education, and one that shaped his method and style.

In spite of this widespread and indeed natural connection between the humanist lawyers and the acceptance of the Reformation, it is among these same lawyers that we find some of the earliest expressions of dissillusionment with the doctrines of the Reform.[31] The very scholars

[30] On Gribaldi Mofa and the Sozzini, see D. Cantimori, *Gli eretici Italiani* (Florence, 1939).

[31] Alfred Hartmann, ed., *Die Amerbachkorrespondenz,* 5 vols. (Basel, 1942–1958), III, nos. 962, 963.

who had been the first to develop and apply a new method for understanding the meaning of ancient authoritative texts were also the first to see its limitations when it was carried too far. Such compilations as the Bible and the *Code of Civil Law,* which had been intricately entwined with the institutional experience of Western civilization, could not be understood by resorting to the tools of philology and grammar alone. In the second part of the sixteenth century a significant number of the greatest professors of civil and canon law turned to the defense of the medieval commentators whom their predecessors had rejected. We can thus follow in the case of one of the learned professions the passage from radicalism to conservatism, from an initial contribution to a great ideological revolution to the exercise of a steadying influence on the acceptance of its consequences.

IV

FIDES ET ERUDITIO

ERASMUS AND THE
STUDY OF HISTORY

THE first work of Erasmus to appear in print was a letter in praise of a history of France and its author.[1] At the beginning of October 1495, Erasmus, who had recently arrived in Paris[2] to study for a doctor's degree in theology, was trying to make his way in the literary world. He appears to have introduced himself almost at once to Robert Gaguin, whose history, the *Compendium de origine et gestis Francorum,* was then being printed. There were some brief exchanges, of which we catch the tone from those of Gaguin's replies that have survived. Erasmus's flattery bought him an opportunity to insert his letter at the end of Gaguin's book before it was published and thus to reach the notice of the literary world through the established fame of the older scholar.

Robert Gaguin[3] was then at the height of his reputa-

---

[1] P. S. Allen, ed., *Opus epistolarum Des. Erasmi Roterodami,* 12 vols. (Oxford, 1906–1958), I, no. 45.

[2] On the date of Erasmus's arrival in Paris see the discussion prefixed to Allen, I, no. 43.

[3] For the biographical details on Gaguin, see the "Notice biographique," in *Roberti Gaguini epistole et orationes,* L. Thuasne, ed. (Paris, 1904), I, 6–168.

tion. Born in 1433, he had led a diversified life in which he distinguished himself in the church, in diplomacy, and in literature. General of the Trinitarian Order, dean of the faculty of law at the University of Paris, he had frequently been employed by Louis XI and Charles VIII on diplomatic missions in Italy, Spain, and England. One of the purposes to which his order was devoted was the recovery of captives from the infidel, and since the fulfillment of this aim also required expeditions abroad, he was able to combine his ecclesiastical with his secular missions. This active career in the service of the Church and State was balanced by a life of study and writing. His literary interests had been shaped by the influence of Italian humanist teaching. Although he knew little or no Greek, he tried in a variety of ways to apply in his own work the lessons of both form and content that he had learned from Latin history and literature. As a young man he had been a careful student of the *Aeneid,* and his own manuscript copy with his marginal notes survives. The vision of the destiny of Aeneas and the mission of imperial Rome took on an added meaning for a Frenchman in the royal service in the days of Louis XI and Charles VIII. Historians and publicists had endowed the first line of the French kings with a genealogy going back to Troy. The domain of the French crown had more than doubled in area and the first great expeditions to Italy in pursuit of the Neapolitan claim were preparing; it seemed that an imperial destiny was also opening before the French monarchy.

The possibility of historical parallels, recurrences of the great deeds of the ancients, cyclical repetitions of typical situations, seems to have occurred to Gaguin although he never developed it into what we should call a philosophy of history. He had been one of the earliest collaborators of Fichet and Heynlin in the work of the Sorbonne press. The third work to issue from this press was an edition of Sallust. In it was printed a little poem by Gaguin on the rebellion and approaching ruin of Charles of Burgundy. The analogy is explicit between the conspiracy of Catiline and the revolt of a great noble against the French monarchy. A sense of the relevance of ancient history was also manifest in the works Gaguin chose to translate. In 1485 he translated into French the *Commentaries* of Caesar and in 1493 the third decade of Livy.

Twice Gaguin petitioned the crown to be named royal historiographer. In the first of these requests, addressed to the chancellor, he emphasized the fact that there had been no skilled writers of French history in Latin although there had been many who had written in the vulgar tongue. Accordingly, the reputation of the French with other nations had suffered. Only in a universal language could the great deeds of the French become a permanent possession. For patriotic reasons he urged the appointment of a qualified historian.[4]

In the second letter he pointed out the examples of virtue and glory, the triumphs over incredible adversity, that could be collected from the reign of Louis XI. He complained that no one had celebrated in literature the virtues of the French kings, who were not inferior to the Caesars. "Nicias and Alcibiades and Hannibal are glorious names but there are more effective examples from our

[4] *Ibid.,* I, no. 23.

own and not from an alien history." There is a justification
not only for remote but also for recent and contemporary
history. He pleaded with the king for a pension and suggested that the great history that he projected would not
be written without pecuniary rewards. Aristotle was sub-
sidized by Alexander and Virgil by Augustus.[5]

On neither of these occasions was the request granted,
but Gaguin's devotion to the monarchy was proof against
any disappointment. He went ahead with his history and
worked on it for years without any subsidy. Had he been
on the official payroll the result could hardly have been
less critical of the growth of the French monarchy. The
Compendium de origine et gestis Francorum was one of
the first attempts to apply to the history of a modern
people methods and conclusions derived from a study of
the great historians of antiquity. The history was written
frankly to prove the point that Gaguin had made in his
letters that "there are more effective examples from our
own history." Since this was the principle, the author had
to be sure that his examples were effective, and the result
was the glorification of the heroes of French history. The
portrait of Charles VIII, who was then reigning, is hardly
more realistic than that of the legendary Pharamond. This
was the work, finally ready to appear in 1495, which was
the object of Erasmus's praise. In spite of his ulterior purposes in composing the letter, Erasmus found it expedient
to say something on the nature of history as well as on
the character of the historian.

He begins by praising Gaguin's talents and motives.
"No other motive than devotion to your country led you

[5] *Ibid.,* I, no. 30.

to undertake this task." This patriotism springs from a sense of piety that all can admire. The reputation of the French has not hitherto been equal to their virtue, and Italy has conquered in literature although not in arms. (It is to be remembered that this letter was written at the time when Charles VIII was returning from the first Italian expedition and the impression made by the news of his original victories over the Italians was still fresh.) Erasmus even quotes a letter from the Italian humanist Filelfo to an earlier Charles of France to show that the French kingdom is inheriting the political succession of the Roman empire and will be the great bulwark of Europe against the Turk. In spite of her great political achievements and her historic destiny, however, France has hitherto lacked a Livy or a Sallust, and without a talented historian the greatest deeds will fall into oblivion. The purpose of history is to perpetuate the virtuous accomplishments of great men, and their fame will be higher in proportion to the genius of the historians who write about them. The two qualities which are especially to be sought in a historian are trustworthiness (*fides*) and learning (*eruditio*). Confidence in the integrity of an author adds a greater plausibility to his account of the course of events, and the genius of a really learned writer may make what is obscure illustrious and what is humble noteworthy; it may even add to the reputation of what is already famous. A historian, then, should combine learning and veracity with literary skill, and he finds his highest duty in the recording of the history of his fatherland. All these qualities Erasmus discovered of course in Gaguin, and the letter concludes with a brief summary of his life and a flattering elaboration on his intellect and character.[6]

It might have been supposed from the evidence of this first published work that Erasmus put a high value on the cultivation of historical studies according to Gaguin's plan and that he would follow in his own work the example of the model he alleged had made such an impression on him. In actual fact, however, Erasmus in his subsequent career and writing revealed very little interest in the kind of history he here praised so extravagantly.

In the first place, nothing was more antipathetic to Erasmus in his maturity than the celebration of the deeds and mission of a particular people in the European community of nations. He was attached to no national tradition, and we cannot imagine him writing a "national" history.[7] Although he probably knew several vernacular tongues, he always refused to use them either in speech or in writing and more than once got into trouble for this intransigence. He resisted every attempt by the national monarchs and even by the emperor to get him into their service, and he preserved his independence by living for the most part in the communes of the Netherlands, Switzerland, and Germany. Basel, Louvain, and Freiburg remained always more congenial to him than Paris, London, or Rome. It is true that he had a keen sense of the differences among the great national groups of the European world and his letters were full of sharp insights and observations on what we should call national charac-

---

[6] Allen, I, no. 45.

[7] See J. Huizinga, "Erasmus über Vaterland und Nationen," in *Gedenkschrift zum 400 Todestage des Erasmus von Rotterdam* (Basel, 1936).

teristics.[8] This is apparent in a well-known passage of his most famous satire. Folly in the course of her oration recognizes among the forms of self-love the collective self-flattery of national groups:

And now I see that it is not only in individual men that nature has implanted self-love. She implants a kind of it as a common possession in the various races and even cities. By this token the English claim, besides a few other things, good looks, music, and the best eating as their special properties. The Scots flatter themselves on the score of high birth and royal blood, not to mention their dialectical skill. Frenchmen have taken all politeness for their province; though the Parisians, brushing all others aside, also award themselves the prize for theology. The Italians usurp *belles-lettres* and eloquence; and they all flatter themselves that they alone, of all mortal men, are not barbarians. In this particular point of happiness the Romans stand highest, still dreaming pleasantly of ancient Rome. The Venetians are blessed with a belief in their own nobility. The Greeks as well as being the founders of the learned disciplines vaunt themselves upon their titles to the famous heroes of old. The Turks, and that whole rabble of the truly barbarous, claim praise for their religion, laughing at Christianity as superstitious. And what is much more pleasant, the Jews are still awaiting their own Messiah, and even today hold on to their Moses with might and main. Spaniards yield to no one in martial reputation. Germans take pride in their great stature and their knowledge of magic.[9]

In the case of Erasmus, however, this kind of dispassionate observation of the differences among the claims of the great national groups at the beginning of the sixteenth century was not accompanied by the growth of

[8] See, for example, Allen, I, no. 103.
[9] Erasmus, *The Praise of Folly,* H. H. Hudson, tr. (Princeton, 1941), p. 61.

any sense of allegiance. The scholar who looked back to the culture of antiquity and the piety of early Christianity was indifferent to the extravagant claims of the national monarchies. Like his friend More, but to an even greater degree, Erasmus was an internationalist; when he thought about contemporary politics at all he kept steadily before his eyes the interests of the *res publica Christiana* and not those of any one parochial group. In an age when nationalism was beginning its greatest triumphs both cultural and political, the foremost scholar of the age neither really understood nor approved it.

Erasmus had, therefore, no sympathy for modern national history, although this was the very basis of the work of Gaguin which he had pretended in 1495 to admire so much. Aside from nationalism, however, there was the broader question of the nature and value of historical studies. Here again there is a striking contrast with the phrases of 1495. All his life Erasmus wrote a great deal on the subject of education, but his formal remarks about history are brief, scattered, and conventional.

In 1511, shortly after finishing the *Praise of Folly,* he composed and published the *De copia verborum ac rerum,* a work whose purpose may be described by saying that it was for the study of Latin in its day roughly an equivalent to Fowler's *Modern English Usage.* It supplied both schoolboys and intended authors with variations in vocabulary, grammatical usages, and tricks of style and rhetoric. As the result of his careful studies in the Latin language and literature for many years, it succeeded to the place previously occupied by Valla's *Elegantiae,* which Erasmus himself had regarded as indispensable for a writer. The

De copia contains a few incidental comments about history. In discussing devices for increasing the interest and variety of narrative description, Erasmus commits himself to the use of imaginary direct discourse by the historian. If we do not know what was actually said on a given past occasion, we are entitled to imagine what ought to have been said. This is the practice of the greatest of poets—Erasmus cites the speeches of Priam and Hecuba to dissuade Hector from going into battle, the appeal of Andromache, and Hector's reply. He continues: "Nor is there anything more admirable in the writers of history, for in the opinion of all it is permitted to historians to invent speeches for individuals." [10] This general rule is followed by an interesting reservation: Erasmus permits himself to doubt whether the same latitude is allowed to historians of Christianity, but he recalls examples from the lives of the martyrs where the practice of antiquity was followed. Except for raising this doubt Erasmus does not suggest departing from standard classical and humanist practice.

The great tradition of "invented" speeches had been inaugurated in Greek historical writing and was maintained and developed by the Romans and their successors. In Thucydides such speeches had served a genuinely dramatic purpose, but many of his successors made them occasions for dramatic flourishes and illustrations of their command of style.[11] In most humanist historical writing of the fifteenth century the device of imaginary direct

[10] Erasmus, *Opera omnia,* J. LeClerc, ed., 10 vols. in 11 (Leyden, 1703–1706), I, col. 106D.

[11] See Sir Richard Jebb, "The Speeches of Thucydides," in *Essays and Addresses* (Cambridge, 1907), pp. 359–443. I owe this reference to

discourse was used not only to conform to rhetorical rules but also to construct idealized portraits. In this way individual historical characters came to exemplify abstract virtues and vices and thus to serve as material for moral instruction. A great gulf separated the purpose of this use of direct discourse from that of a realist like Guicciardini, who, in his masterpiece covering the years of Erasmus's mature life, used the same rhetorical device to underline the ironic difference between what men said and what they did. Erasmus's position in the *De copia* is that of traditional humanism. Nor does he reveal any awareness of the possibility of a new dimension in historical writing of the kind which was emerging in the Italian realist school.

History conceived as philosophy teaching by example was the view Erasmus also adopted in other works when he had occasion to consider the place of history in education. In 1516 he wrote for the future Charles V the *Institutio principis christiani.* The emphasis is entirely upon the moral instruction of the young prince, and Erasmus appears to be very doubtful whether history has any real place in that instruction. History can in fact be dangerous. "A boy who is wild and impetuous by nature would easily be incited to tyranny, if without forewarning he should read about Achilles, Alexander the Great, Xerxes or Julius Caesar." Even worse than examples drawn from ancient history are the legends of King Arthur, "poorly done, stupid and fit for old wives' tales so that it would be more advisable to put in one's time

Professor Hajo Holborn of Yale University, who was kind enough to read my essay in manuscript.

reading the comedies or the poets instead of nonsense of that sort." [12] Erasmus recommended to the prince a course of reading which began with the *Proverbs* of Solomon, *Ecclesiastes,* and the *Book of Wisdom,* and continued with the *Moralia* of Plutarch and the works of Seneca. Finally the studious prince was to come to Aristotle's *Politics,* Cicero's *Offices,* and Plato's *Republic.* Erasmus protests that he does not deny that a great fund of wisdom may be gathered from a reading of the historians, but unless they are read with discretion they may give counsel which will lead to destruction. Sometimes, however, bad examples may be turned to good. If historians are read selectively, the lives of wicked tyrants may be more instructive than those of mediocre princes.[13]

Elsewhere Erasmus repeated even more conventional views on the value of examples from history. In the *De conscribendis epistolis* he discussed the way history from the most ancient times down to the most recent can be utilized.[14] In a letter written in 1527 Erasmus advised a young German, Valentine Fürster, to spend a large part of his time on ethical and historical writers because of the usefulness of the examples he could get from them. Livy, Tacitus, and Plutarch are especially mentioned.[15] But it is clear here as well as elsewhere that when historians and moral philosophers are mentioned together, the latter are preferred by Erasmus. Ancient histories are better than modern, and sacred history as revealed in the books of the Bible is infinitely above profane history.

[12] Erasmus, *The Education of a Christian Prince,* Lester K. Born, tr. (New York, 1936), pp. 200–201.
[13] *Ibid.* [14] *Opera omnia,* I, col. 389F. [15] Allen, VI, no. 1798.

"Compare," says one of the speakers in the *Ciceronianus*, "Herodotus and his fables with Moses; compare the history of the creation and the exodus from Egypt with the fables of Diodorus. Compare the books of the Jews and Kings with Titus Livy who is often inconsistent with himself in his account of things—so far is he from a strict adherence to truth." [16] In any case the study of history whether sacred or profane is merely introductory to a greater purpose. It ought not to be rejected because it is the basis of allegory and leads us on to the discovery of a more abstract sense.[17] Eternal unchanging truth is hidden behind the temporal flux of the historical world.

On the basis of this evidence it would be easy to conclude that the intellectual interests of Erasmus were essentially unhistorical. He seems to have repeated the ordinary commonplaces of humanist discourse. Who would not agree that poetry, moral philosophy, and sacred history were to be preferred to secular annals? And if history had a function at all, what else could it be but that of philosophy teaching by example? Such attitudes were the product of considering history as so many pieces of historical literature—Thucydides, Livy, Tacitus, etc. Insofar as these judgments and opinions implied any general view at all of the nature of history, it was one founded upon classical and cyclical ideas. Human nature remained substantially unchanged; the same accidents could happen to individuals as to peoples, again and again. In some expressions Erasmus seems almost to agree with Machiavelli's judgment on the repetitive course of human affairs.

[16] *Opera omnia*, V, col. 470C.   [17] *Opera omnia*, I, col. 998A.

Certainly the view he most commonly expressed about the value of history seems far removed from the enthusiasm of the letter to Gaguin. Not only did Erasmus not write any formal histories himself; what he said about them seems conventional and disappointing.

Yet such a conclusion would not be warranted. Side by side with his appeals to traditional humanist opinion, there exists in Erasmus's writings a different and much deeper understanding of the historical process. Rarely expressed and then only indirectly, it is implicit in the aims and achievements of his whole scholarly career.

Like his conventional views on the value of historical studies, Erasmus owed this understanding in part to his Italian humanist predecessors, but it was also a specific product of his own genius. Viewed as a whole, the fusion of the individual and traditional elements in his thought produced a philosophy of history significantly related to the ideals of both the Renaissance and the Reformation.

The first element in that philosophy was a sense of perspective on the classical past. This had been one of the distinctive contributions of Petrarchan humanism, developed and refined by the scholarship of the fifteenth century. Historians of art have pointed out the importance of this phenomenon in the transformation of iconography. In medieval classical revivals there had usually been a sharp separation between plastic expression and literary tradition, so that biblical personages appeared in classical dress and antique gods and goddesses as contemporary knights and ladies. Beginning roughly about the time of Petrarch, the new historical sense began to restore to a literary theme its proper historical content.[18] The same phenomenon was also manifest in the treatment of many literary and philosophical texts. In this development the study of legal texts was particularly important. The careful and continuing investigation of the meaning of certain terms in the great source collections of Roman law led ultimately to the discovery that although words remained the same they could stand for very different things at different times. There is a good deal of evidence to support the conclusion that a keen sense of the historical differences between the Roman world and the European Middle Ages first emerged among scholars of the law. Aided by increasingly refined philological techniques, they developed a novel awareness of a historical process in which elements of change and continuity were mingled; the result was a consciousness of perspective in time which had been missing in the Middle Ages.[19]

This realization—as yet incomplete—that various cultural characteristics "belonged together" in a given historical epoch was accompanied at the same time not only by a perception of the distance of such an epoch from the contemporary world but also by a sense of the "deadness" of the past compared with the living present. Men looked back on the glorious Roman past with nostalgia and with vain longing to establish a more intimate contact with the men and the ways of thought of this vanished age. This

[18] For a discussion of this phenomenon see E. Panofsky, "Renaissance and Renascences," *Kenyon Review* 6:201–306 (1944), as well as the same author's *Studies in Iconology: Humanistic Themes in the Art of the Renaissance* (New York, 1939).

[19] See Roberto Weiss, *Il primo secolo dell'umanesimo* (Rome, 1949), p. i.

is the feeling we have seen voiced by Petrarch in the letters he addressed to the great authors of antiquity.[20]

The perspective of humanism extended from the eye of the fifteenth-century observer to the Greek and Roman past, but the civilization of the ancient world in the distance was bathed in an ever stronger and clearer light while the foreground was dark and the middle distance still more obscure. This view was shared also by many of the humanist historians of the Quattrocento who were moved to write their histories largely because they wished to have their own times and the deeds of their great men live in the future in the same way as the Greco-Roman age and the heroes of antiquity had come down to them. Saved from the ravages of time, examples from the present, as Gaguin had pointed out, could be as instructive as those of the past. The fact that the remote past was so much better known than recent years was primarily due to its having been illuminated by literary genius. History and eloquence could therefore prevent the destruction by time of the great deeds of the present.

From this view of the purpose of historical writing there often followed the conclusion that the nature of the historical process was a repetitive pattern. All examples illustrated the same virtues and the same vices. Human nature was unchanging and the same accidents happened to different peoples. This was one current in humanist historical thought powerfully expressed in Machiavelli, and we have seen that Erasmus in some of his writing appears to share this view. Many humanists built them-

[20] Petrarch, *Epistolae de rebus familiaribus et variae*, J. Fracassetti, ed., 3 vols. (Florence, 1859–1863), III, 282.

selves a dream world in which the word could be taken for the reality. This was conspicuously true of the so-called Ciceronians at the beginning of the sixteenth century. They prided themselves on purifying their vocabulary of any base modernisms and found their ultimate linguistic authority in the canon of Cicero's works. Although they managed to convince at least themselves that by applying the language of Cicero to the contemporary world they were bringing back to life the great age of Rome, they never perceived that they were dealing with language not life. The outcome of their cult ironically defeated their intention: instead of revivifying the past they turned Latin from a living to a dead language. In the general humanist tradition the Ciceronians exemplified the most limited view of the relation between past and present and the most literal acceptance of the possibility of historical recurrence.

There was, however, in this tradition another and contrasting attitude toward history which emphasized the unique rather than the recurrent and the linear rather than the cyclical. The nostalgia of Petrarch himself, powerful as it was, did not yield to the illusion that an age dead and gone could be made to come to life again in its entirety. That element in humanist thought which emphasized the sense of historical perspective and the ineluctable and irrecoverable passage of time received continuous expression. Although Erasmus, as we have seen, was neither philosophical nor discursive on the subject of history, one of the best examples of the conflict between the two views is provided by his attack on the Ciceronians.

His dialogue *Ciceronianus* was written in 1529. The conception of linguistic purity developed by Bembo and other Italians that maintained that one ought never to use a word which had not occurred in the corpus of Ciceronian writing seemed absurd to Erasmus, and he attacked it with spirit and irony. One passage is particularly relevant to the argument on history. Nosoponus, the character in the dialogue who defends the use of pure Ciceronian lauguage, is persuaded by his opponent, Bulephorus, to agree that language must be relevant to contemporary life. Bulephorus then asks: "But can it be maintained that the situation of the present century is at all like that in which Cicero lived? On the contrary, religion, the empire, the magistrates, the government, laws, customs, ordinary pursuits, and the very appearance of men have all changed." When Nosoponus admits this, then Bulephorus wants to know how anyone can possibly demand in all things the use of the language of Cicero:

Let the man who makes such a demand first give us back Rome itself as it once was, the Senate and the *curia*, the *Patres conscripti*, the equestrian order, the people divided in tribes and centuries; let him bring back the colleges of augurs and *aruspices*, the *pontifex maximus*, the *flamines*, and the vestal virgins, the aediles, the praetors, the tribunes of the *plebs*, the consuls, dictators, caesars, *comitia*, *leges*, *senatusconsulta*, *plebiscita*, statues, triumphs, ovations, supplications, shrines, temples and seats of the gods, the sacred rites, the gods and goddesses, the Capitoline, and the sacred fire; let him return the provinces, colonies, free towns, and allies of the master city. But indeed since the whole scene of human affairs has been overturned, who today can talk sensibly unless he uses language very different from that of Cicero? Wherever I turn my eyes I see all things changed, I stand before another stage and I behold a different play, nay, even a different world.[22]

In these words Erasmus seems to be thinking about history in a way that anticipates the historicism of a much later period. For many of his contemporaries there was between past and present a substantial continuity which extended not only to institutions but also to manners and customs and even to the details of daily life. Beyond the philological labors of a few scholars the concept of anachronism hardly existed. A Lorenzo Valla discussing the authenticity of the *Donation of Constantine* could urge among other arguments against it the fact that the document refers to the imperial crown whereas in reality in this period the Roman emperors wore a fillet and not a crown.[23] But this idea of what was historically "correct" had not begun to penetrate all realms of thought even among the intellectuals, to say nothing of the populace at large. Down through the eighteenth century historical characters appeared on the stage in contemporary costume, and people did not demand an "archaeological" correctness in the furniture of their historical dramas. Erasmus, on the other hand, at least when he wrote the passage quoted above, was arguing against anachronisms. The course of history was like that of a single life. "There is only one age in which you can learn," Erasmus wrote to a young student. "It will never come back." [24] Cicero lived in another world, immeasurably remote, and this world

[22] *Opera omnia,* I, col. 992C ff. My translation.
[23] Lorenzo Valla, *On the Donation of Constantine,* Christopher Coleman, tr. (New Haven, 1922), p. 107.   [24] Allen, IV, no. 1198.

could not be recovered by the simple device of putting on blinders and agreeing to call things by their wrong names.

Yet, if the past could not be thus recreated in its entirety, it could at least be accurately known, and the provision of this knowledge was the chief task of the scholar. By his faithful erudition the important texts of the classical and the Christian tradition could be understood in their true historical context. In order to understand a text it was necessary first to purity it of the corrupting influences of time and error and, second, to apply to the reading of it a sound philological knowledge. Only in this way could the true meaning of sources be interpreted, and only through sources could history itself, whether of ideas or institutions, be understood.

This aim is the theme set forth in the prefaces to Erasmus's greatest and most important work of scholarship, the *Novum Instrumentum*. Again and again Erasmus emphasized the necessity of a return to the sources. "He is no Platonist who does not read the works of Plato and no Christian, still less a theologian, who cannot read the Gospel." [25] In his *Methodus* and in the *Ratio seu compendium verae theologiae* he laid down principles for the study of scriptural texts. These included not only mastery of the three languages, Latin, Greek, and Hebrew, and a knowledge of grammar and rhetoric, but also knowledge of nature. ("What will it profit you to utter a syllogism on the crocodile . . . if you do not know whether a crocodile is a kind of plant or animal?") [26] It was also necessary

[25] Erasmus, *Ausgewählte Werke,* Hajo and Annemarie Holborn, eds. (Munich, 1933), p. 144.   [26] *Ibid.,* p. 186.

to know the institutions and customs of the society in which Jesus lived and taught. All this amounts to what we should call the historical explication of a text, and this was the method essentially applied in the *Novum Instrumentum* and the editions of the Church Fathers.

Examples of the uses of this method which might be cited are many. The celebrated omission of the text of I John 5: 7, on the Three Heavenly Witnesses is only the most elementary application of the idea of establishing a text from the best manuscript tradition. The fact is that not one of the Greek manuscripts to which Erasmus had access contained this text and he was simply unable under these circumstances to include it. When challenged he agreed, perhaps rather hastily, to restore it if a manuscript authority were produced. One was forthcoming and Erasmus kept his promise and restored the text in the edition of 1519, although it now seems clear that the manuscript he was offered was forged for the occasion.[27]

In a still wider field, however, than that of a strict adherence to a manuscript tradition, Erasmus showed his grasp of a sense of history. The notes to the New Testament and the prefaces to the Fathers contain a wealth of historical analysis anticipating the achievement of a later age. Again and again he inquires into the precise meaning of a word in a passage and the sense of the passage in relation to its context. "I consider that this is the principal key to the understanding of scriptural difficulty, to investigate what he who speaks is thinking about, especially in the case of Paul, who is most free in disputation, rushing

[27] See the discussion of this text in Preserved Smith, *Erasmus* (New York, 1923), pp. 165–166.

now hither, now thither, so that as Origen says, the reader hardly understands where he came in and where he is going." [28]

The fruit of this method is to be seen in a more extensive area in such productions as the discourse on the itineraries of St. Peter and St. Paul[29] and the *Life of St. Jerome*.[30] Here is historical reconstruction built on the sources, with full recognition of the differences that separate the ages of St. Peter or St. Jerome from Erasmus's own time in the sixteenth century. In announcing his method at the beginning of the *St. Jerome,* Erasmus rejects the miraculous as well as incredible feats of piety such as have been ascribed to subsequent saints. If examples of piety are to be related they are to be such as were known in the first age of the Christian Church. "Although the artisan can bring out the sparkle and lustre of any gem, yet no imitation ever attains the inherent quality of a gem. Truth has its own energy which no artifice can equal." [31] These expressions and others like them are as remote from the method that allowed the insertion of imaginary direct discourse as the achievement of Erasmus was from that of Gaguin. With such a work as the *Life of St. Jerome* we are already at the beginning of the principles of modern historical criticism.

The distance between the letter on Gaguin and the *Life of St. Jerome* does not wholly represent a progress from youth to age. In reality throughout the whole body

---

[28] *Opera omnia,* VI, col. 701B. My translation.

[29] *Opera omnia,* VI, cols. 425–432.

[30] W. Ferguson, ed., *Des. Erasmi Roterodami Opuscula* (The Hague, 1933), pp. 134–190.

[31] *Ibid.,* p. 136.

of Erasmus's work there coexist two different views on history, each one owing much to his humanist predecessors but fundamentally incompatible with the other. The one was founded on the view that the chief function of history was to furnish examples of virtue and vice, that is, illustrations of timeless truths applied to the recurrent pattern of situations in which men found themselves involved. The other emphasized what could be learned from a unique historical evolution. The first was an essentially cyclical conception derived originally from the classical philosophers and historians. The second was a linear interpretation resting ultimately on the implications of the Christian religion. The difference between the two approaches may be crudely put by viewing it as centering on the point of departure. In the one a student went to history to find examples to illustrate truths derived from other sources, morality, religion, and philosophy. In the other he went to history to find out what truths could be elicited from it to apply to an understanding of morality, religion, and philosophy. When Erasmus talked about history in the abstract or as a part of an educational scheme, he tended to make use of the first or classical idea, but a whole lifetime of study of classical and Christian literature illustrated his adherence to the second. Like many great historians before and since, what he said *about* history was often singularly unrelated to what he did when he actually wrote history.

This dualism is apparent in his most comprehensive expressions on the subject of historical change and the relation between past and present. He is constantly using the expressions *renovatio, restoratio, instauratio.* "It is a better thing to have restored than to have founded." "A genuine and purer literature will come to renewed life." ". . . three of the chief blessings of humanity are about to be restored to her." "Roman law and mathematics are restored." [32] At certain moments, as in the spring of 1517, he appears to have anticipated the imminent return of a golden age almost in the spirit of Virgil's *Fourth Eclogue*. What was the nature of these renewals and restorations? We have already seen that in arguing against the Ciceronians Erasmus rejected the concept of a past which could be recaptured and imitated in its entirety. But if the stage was a different one and the play had never been performed before, it was still possible to hope that the characters might express intellectual and moral qualities of a height equal to or greater than those attained in great ages of the past. Amidst the fluctuations of historical circumstances and constantly changing institutions, learning and piety could be preserved from destruction by time, and the benefits of this achievement could be extended to an ever wider group. Insofar as this happened there would indeed be renewals of a golden age. If the process failed, ignorance and barbarism would be the result. The balance was a delicate one, and the optimism expressed by Erasmus in the years before 1517 was replaced by doubt and despair as he surveyed in his old age the effects of the Reformation.

At the basis of Erasmus's outlook on history was an emphasis on what could be accomplished by the rational faculties of man. His view of history was thus essentially dynamic. Erasmus did not merely postulate the appear-

---

[32] For these expressions, see Allen, II, nos. 384, 541, and 566.

ance now and again of a timeless virtue in the chaos of men's affairs. The qualities which he so admired had themselves been the product of a slow historical growth in the history of mankind. The wisdom of classical antiquity had prepared the way for Christianity. The Christian message was not in contradiction with the classical but in fulfillment of it. In the *Antibarbari* he defended the necessary connection between Christian charity and knowledge. "Without *scientia, caritas* is like a ship without a rudder." [33] This was not a doctrine of progress in anything like the modern sense. The modern doctrine as it was developed in the nineteenth century embraced both man and his environment. Not only was the nature of the individual man capable of steady improvement, but also the social and political institutions and the material circumstances which surrounded him were indefinitely perfectible. Erasmus was interested only incidentally in these institutional surroundings. There had been many stages and many different sets of scenery; unlike the theater, however, when the play was over the sets could not be used again. Erasmus participated in the first results of a genuinely historical outlook when he perceived how different from one another some of these scenes had been. But among the actors there was a certain continuity; there were lessons to be learned. History—the intellectual history of antiquity and early Christianity—showed the conditions for the intellectual and spiritual growth of man. As in time past there had been a development from learning to piety, from classicism to Christianity, so in time present learning could restore piety, and even more—as larger numbers of

[33] *Opera omnia*, X, col. 1718F. Cited in R. Pfeiffer, *Humanitas Erasmiana* (Berlin, 1931), p. 13.

people profited from the methods of learning correctly applied—so the benefits of piety would be ever more widely distributed.

The proposition that there was a connection between piety and the right kind of education reflected the humanist belief in an aristocracy of intellect. Erasmus's educational treatises emphasized the training of that small number who were fitted by birth or intellect to assume positions of responsibility, the young noblemen, the Christian knight, even the future Charles V. If those who were to be the rulers of the world could but be given the proper education, the age of the philosopher kings would arrive. Yet it must also be remembered that the benefits of the new learning were not to be confined to those highly placed by birth or genius. The well-known remarks in the *Paraclesis* in which Erasmus affirmed his desire to have the ploughboy and the housewife know the Gospel and recite the Psalms, show that even in those of the meanest capacity Erasmus felt that knowledge was a necessary condition for piety.[34] He did not share Luther's belief that the simple unlettered peasant might be truly more pious than all the doctors. A program of education which was within the reach of human planning was thus to prepare the way for the greater triumphs of Christianity, both within Europe and in the newly discovered lands that were being brought within the European horizon. In that educational program history as a formal subject was allotted but a small place, but the whole scheme nevertheless depended on Erasmus's conquest of the historical world of antiquity and early Christianity.

In the letter to Gaguin, Erasmus had declared that *fides*

[34] Holborn, eds., *Erasmi Werke*, p. 142.

and *eruditio* were the two qualities most necessary for a good historian. Far more than the man he then praised, Erasmus had realized these qualities in the work of a lifetime. But in another sense and different from what he had intended, his choice of words was significant. The word *fides,* of course, carried for Erasmus the connotations of its use by the ancient rhetoricians and perhaps particularly by Quintilian, who, in the fifth book of his *De oratore,* discusses the nature of argument as a method of proving what is not certain by means of what is certain. This is the Greek *pistis,* which Quintilian translates *probatio* or *fides,* meaning a warrant or security for credibility. Quintilian, however, did not have to consider the senses acquired by *fides* when it was applied to the Christian religion. For a more complete understanding of Erasmus's usage of the term we must therefore look to his immediate intellectual background in the Italian humanists. Among the fifteenth-century Italians, we know that Lorenzo Valla had by far the most direct influence on Erasmus: the impetus indeed for Erasmus's work on the New Testament came from Valla's *Annotationes,* which Erasmus discovered and edited, thus becoming the heir of Valla's historical and critical method. Among Valla's other works Erasmus always paid the highest tribute to the *Elegantiae Linguae Latinae,* and it is precisely in the *Elegantiae* that we find a passage on *fides* which Erasmus may well have had in mind when he spoke of the *fides* of the historian.

Valla agrees that the proper Latin equivalent of *fides* is *probatio,* proof, "whether offered by documents, by arguments or by witnesses. Yet the Christian religion advances less by proof than by persuasion, which is nobler than proof. For often," he continues, "we are not influenced by proof as, for example, when a bad servant, a bad child, or a bad wife, may not agree with an argument which cannot be refuted, but a man who is persuaded acquiesces fully and seeks no further proof. And because *fides* can also be taken for the quality that inspires this kind of belief, rightly is our religion called a faith." [35]

Certainly, in many of his statements on *fides* as applied to historians, Erasmus seems to be thinking of these implications. He speaks of the duty of conserving *cum summa fide* the text of an historian by whose *fide* such an important part of our knowledge of the ancient world has been preserved. Even if he conceived the text of the ancient historian as offering proof, he had certainly moved from proof to persuasion when he proclaimed his belief that *fides* in its religious sense depended on erudition, that the discovery of the significance of the Christian message and the restoration of piety were the products of historical research. The development of a historical consciousness has not always been accompanied by a growth in the sense of freedom or a feeling of confidence in the future; there are some in the modern world who have found the burden of history intolerable, and it has been said that the only logical conclusion to a complete historicism is existentialism. In the Renaissance the emergent sense of history was limited in scope and perhaps for that very reason it supported a confidence in man's capacity to rule his destiny. The thought of Eras-

[35] Lorenzo Valla, *De linguae latinae elegantiae libri sex* (Paris, 1539), f⁰ 175 v⁰. My translation.

mus marks a stage between the medieval lack of awareness of a different past and the later European preoccupation with the concept of development from one state to another. The balance between faith and erudition sustained a bright hope which, though tragically disappointed in Erasmus's own lifetime, persisted as an ideal and shaped the thought of subsequent generations on the relation of Christianity to time and the course of human history.

V

ERASMUS AND THE CAUSE
OF CHRISTIAN HUMANISM
THE LAST YEARS 1529–1536

DESIDERIUS Erasmus of Rotterdam is one of those great figures in intellectual history whose message and significance have been variously interpreted by succeeding generations of students. Even in his own lifetime the judgments upon him were ambiguous and full of contradictions. As the author of most influential works of devotion and instruction, he formulated a conception of Christian piety based on the Gospels and the Epistles of St. Paul and emphasizing the importance of the spirit rather than of the letter; as a scholar he provided the first edition of the Greek text of the New Testament with a new Latin translation as well as many editions of the Church Fathers; as a critic he delivered the sharpest of indictments of many ecclesiastical abuses and hyprocrisies. In all these capacities he was rightly regarded by his contemporaries as one of those most responsible for the Protestant Reformation and yet he repudiated the work of Luther and Zwingli and their followers and was in his old age execrated by most sectors of Protestant opinion. A powerful body of Catholic opinion likewise denounced him for accepting too much rather than too little of

Protestantism. Yet, in the last year of his life, he was offered a cardinal's hat by Pope Paul III.

A longer perspective did nothing to diminish these differing estimates. In spite of the high esteem in which he had been held by all the Renaissance popes, the Council of Trent put on the *Index* a large part of his work, including the notes on the New Testament, the *Paraphrases* of the New Testament, the *Complaint of Peace,* and the *Colloquies.* Protestant opinion continued to regard him as a craven figure who had denied out of cowardice the cause for which he originally fought. In the age when the bitterness of religious controversy was receding, on the threshold of the eighteenth-century enlightenment, Pierre Bayle, by putting the portrait of Erasmus at the frontispiece of his *Historical and Critical Dictionary,* created a new image of Erasmus as a commanding figure in the history of European rationalism.

In the scholarship of our own day the pattern of contradiction has continued. Among recent works on Erasmus one commentator has maintained that all his work was motivated by an attempt, perhaps in part unconscious but none the less real, to attack traditional orthodoxy and in particular the sacraments.[1] Another has hailed Erasmus as genuinely Catholic in spirit and rather to be seen as a precursor of the Counter Reformation than of Protestantism.[2] On the other hand an Italian scholar has attacked the concept of Christian humanism so often applied to the work of Erasmus.[3] This scholar asserts that such a term

[1] E. V. Telle, *Erasme de Rotterdam et le Septième Sacrement: étude d'evangelisme matrimonial au XVIe siècle et contribution a la biographie intellectuelle d'Erasme* (Geneva, 1954).

[2] L. Bouyer, *Autour d'Erasme* (Paris, 1958).

[3] S. A. Nulli, *Erasmo e il Rinascimento* (Milan, 1955).

is without meaning, that one might as well speak of a Catholic geometry or a Christian chemistry. There can be no compromise between the rationalism of the Greek spirit and the other-worldliness of Christianity.

Thus each generation has seen the many-sided figure of Erasmus from a new perspective. Living as we do today in a period of ideological conflict, we perhaps think first of Erasmus as the victim of a tragic situation in which the opposition between two interpretations of the Christian tradition had become ever more polarized. This dilemma became particularly acute in the last years of Erasmus's life when he met increasing pressure to define his relation to Rome and to Wittenberg. In spite of the interest which it offers, however, this last period of Erasmus's life has been less considered by almost all his biographers.[4] In general they have concentrated on the earlier period when the "important" work was done and they pass over the years in which they consider that Erasmus was left behind by the stormy course of events and became a pathetic, hypochondriac, querulous old man. This neglect has in part been due to the fact that P. S. Allen's great edition of the *Letters of Erasmus*, the eleven volumes of which were published over a period of more than fifty years, reached the final volume in 1957 and the invaluable index volume in the following year.[5] Thus, the letters of the latter period were not available even to many of the twentieth-century biographers such as Preserved Smith, Emerton, and Huizinga. As the last

[4] An exception is the recent excellent study by Karl H. Oelrich, *Der späte Erasmus und die Reformation* (Münster, 1961).

[5] P. S. Allen, ed., *Opus Epistolarum Des. Erasmi Roterodami,* 12 vols. (Oxford, 1906–1958).

of these declared in his biography in 1924: "The old Erasmus at Freiburg . . . will only be fully revealed to us when his correspondence with Boniface Amerbach, the friend whom he left behind at Basel, a correspondence not found complete in the older collections, has been edited by Dr. Allen's care. From no period of Erasmus's life, it seems, may so much be gleaned in point of knowledge of his daily habits and thoughts as from these very years." [6] This prediction of a great biographer of Erasmus is confirmed, now that the correspondence has become entirely available, not only in the Allen edition but also from Amerbach's side, in the great edition of the letters of the Amerbach family published at Basel.[7] In these exchanges with his intimate friends we can follow the almost daily reflections of Erasmus on the great issues of the time and we can see also to what an extent Erasmus maintains in his old age the attitudes toward history and tradition that he had developed in his earlier years. Let us begin with the triumph of the Reformation in Basel which marked a turning point in Erasmus's career.

At noon on the 13th of April 1529 there occurred in the city of Basel on the quay near the bridge a scene which marks a significant moment in the intellectual history of the Reformation. Erasmus was taking his departure from Basel. He had long been familiar with the city and it had been his residence for the past eight years. Here his greatest works had been printed and here also he was the leader of a circle whose members included

[6] J. Huizinga, *Erasmus of Rotterdam,* F. Hopman, tr. (London, 1952), p. 176.
[7] A. Hartmann, ed., *Die Amerbachkorrespondenz,* 5 vols. (Basel, 1943–1948).

the elder and the younger Holbein, the Amerbach family, and the Frobens, names associated with the highest achievements of Renaissance culture not only in Switzerland but throughout the Christian world.

During the winter and early spring months of 1529 the Reformation had taken a more violent course in the city. The mob had stormed the cathedral and broken the images and finally the town council had officially adopted the doctrines of the Reform and established an order of worship devised by Oecolampadius. In spite of his work and his friends, Erasmus felt that he could no longer remain in the city without violence to the conclusions of his conscience and to his reputation in the eyes of the world. After some consideration of where he might best find a refuge he chose Freiburg-im-Breisgau, a city under imperial jurisdiction only 40 miles removed from Basel. It was the seat of a university where Erasmus had many friends, chief among whom was Ulrich Zasius, the great jurist. To this city he was given a safe conduct by the Emperor's brother, Ferdinand of Hungary, and it was arranged that he should inhabit the house that had been built in 1516 for the Emperor Maximilian. In the first weeks of April he sent his books and his luggage ahead of him to Freiburg. In the last days he had an interview with Oecolampadius who tried to dissuade him from his intention but in vain. The interview, however, was amicable enough and it is to the credit of the Basel Reformers that no impediment was put in Erasmus's way. He had originally intended to take his departure secretly from a landing place somewhat below the city. This, however, the fathers of the town council refused to allow, and

Basel's most eminent citizen, fleeing from an order which he could no longer accept, was accompanied to the landing stage by a delegation of the town council to wish him well.[8]

There are two letters at the very beginning of the Freiburg period which are of the greatest significance in defining Erasmus's religious position in the year 1529.

The first was written to Louis Ber on March 30, 1529, on the eve of Erasmus's departure from Basel. Ber was an old friend who had studied theology in Paris and then returned to Basel where he taught at the University, eventually becoming rector. He was so little in sympathy with the Reformation that he had preceded Erasmus in leaving Basel and had found a position on the faculty at Freiburg. Ber was a man whose Catholic orthodoxy had never been questioned and who had, in fact, distinguished himself by fighting against the publication of Lutheran books. In this letter Erasmus tells about his impending move to Freiburg and points out that he has already sent his heavy baggage ahead and is only waiting to deal with some matters of the printing press before he starts on his journey. He deplores the condition of the times and the perversion of the Evangel to the cause of sedition. He thinks it probable that God has brought these calamities as a punishment for the morals of the age. Reviewing his own past scholarly activity and its connection with the new religious doctrines, Erasmus professes that he has studied languages and literature for no other good

[8] On the Reformation in Basel, see R. Wackernagel, *Geschichte der Stadt Basel,* 3 vols. in 4 (Basel, 1907–1924), III, 463–524, and Theodore Burckhardt-Biedermann, *Bonifacius Amerbach und die Reformation* (Basel, 1894). On Erasmus's departure see Allen, VIII, no. 2149 and the citations there given in Allen's introductory note.

than for the advancement of a knowledge of theology, that indeed his only desire has been a clergy who would know more of the sources of Christianity and the Fathers of the Church. He never wanted scholastic theology removed but only purified of its excrescences. He had exhorted monks to be more truly what they professed, that is, dead to the interests of the world, and had urged them to put less trust in outward ceremony and more in true piety. "Can this," he says, "be taken as a hatred of monasticism?" "I have often," he continued, "beseeched popes, cardinals, and bishops to turn to apostolic piety, but never did it come into my mind that any of them should be removed from their dignities. Never have I taught that the constitutions and observances of the Church should be despised, but I have emphasized the precepts of God and shown the way from ceremonies to better things. And if in these matters the negligence of men has broken out, I have shown in what respect it can be corrected, a thing which the Church has often done in the past. There is no sacrament of the Church which I have not always venerated, although about matrimony I notice there are different opinions among the old authorities. Of the sacrament of confession I never had any doubt. Of abrogating the mass I never even dreamed. In any scruples about the eucharist I am accustomed to acquiesce in the judgment of the Catholic Church. I have always uniquely abhorred sects and schisms. Nor up to now have I given my adherence to any faction nor have I collected any disciples for myself, but if I have attained any I give them over to Christ." [9]

In the letter to Ber, Erasmus thus makes a full pro-

[9] Allen, VIII, no. 2136. My translation.

fession of his Catholic belief, particularly emphasizing his commitment to the authority of the Church. On the crucial question of how the authority of the Church was to be defined Erasmus does not extend himself. He frequently hopes that matters seriously in debate will be referred to a council but he speaks respectfully of the authority wielded by the holder of the See of Peter. It is clear, however, that in opposition to the Reformers' appeal to Scripture alone, Erasmus submitted to the authority of tradition, without perhaps facing even in his own mind, the question of how tradition was to be defined and interpreted.

Three years later, in March 1532, Erasmus wrote a comparable letter to a Protestant. His correspondent this time was Martin Bucer, the Reformer of Strasbourg. Bucer had already distinguished himself as a member of the moderate party and had three years before tried to reconcile the views of Luther and Zwingli on the eucharist. His moderation and his good will kept him in correspondence with Erasmus and he obviously earnestly hoped to bring Erasmus into association with his own ideas and his own work of reformation at Strasbourg. The exchange with Bucer had been evoked by the publication of Sebastian Franck's *Chronica* at Strasbourg in 1531. Erasmus apparently thought the book had been produced by Bucer and he complained to the magistrates of Strasbourg that his position had been incorrectly represented. Evidently Bucer then wrote to Erasmus reviewing the history of Erasmus's relation with the Reformation. Bucer's letter is no longer extant but Erasmus's long reply on March 2, 1532, answers Bucer's points paragraph by paragraph. The tone is throughout amicable and courteous. He says to Bucer, "You are persuaded that the doctrine that you profess is the doctrine of Christ. If I were equally so persuaded no one would profess your doctrine more freely than I." He asserts the simplicity and purity of the philosophy of Christ and discusses the relation of the Reformers with the princes. Although Bucer had tried to excuse the necessity of innovations in liturgy and ritual, Erasmus points out the lengths to which the evangelical party has gone in demolishing even the most pious statues and paintings. He again discusses the definition of the eucharist and again asserts his orthodoxy. Throughout there is a tone of sadness: "I have lived a long time, what remains is not life, but a slow death." He concludes by pointing out that his former friend Wolfgang Capito has now married, and he feels that this departure from traditional orthodoxy, since Capito was in orders, further undermines his confidence in the leaders of the Reformation party. He feels no such confidence in the integrity of either Capito or Bucer himself as would lead him to submit his soul to their direction, but prays that Christ may inspire his opponents with wise counsels. This epistle, in effect, constitutes Erasmus's farewell to such hopes as he had earlier entertained that any good might come from the movement begun by Luther.[10]

The Reformation was again repudiated and Catholic orthodoxy again declared with varying degrees of emphasis in other letters written during these years. Erasmus entered into the defense not only of doctrines but also of institutions which his own previous work had

[10] Allen, IX, no. 2615. My translation.

seemed to undermine. In February 1533 he wrote a letter to his friend John of Heemstede, a Carthusian monk in Louvain, dedicating to him an edition of the *Life of the Blessed Haymo*. Haymo was a ninth-century monk who had been a pupil of Alcuin; a contemporary manuscript had come into Erasmus's possession and he decided to prepare an edition of this little work of Carolingian hagiography, using the occasion to declare his faith in the ideals of monasticism. Through the dedication the monastic virtues as exemplified by Haymo in the ninth century were linked to those of Erasmus's contemporary and friend. The preface gives an account of the beauty and purity of early monasticism and maintains that it is only the evil lives of certain monks of the more recent period which has caused the institution to fall into disrepute. If the true ideals of monasticism are considered, "who," says Erasmus, "will not love these men who . . . have dedicated themselves entirely to God? . . . They repay misdeeds with benefactions . . . the closer they come to the peak of perfection, the more they consider themselves the lowest, although in truth they are the flowers and gems of the church . . . they bring before us a kind of image of the celestial city in which they perpetually sing the praises of God." Erasmus continues in still more extravagant language to ask how laymen dare to think ill of those who in effect watch over their daily lives. "Do you profess yourself a Christian," he says, addressing an imaginary layman, "and yet turn from those who are most like Christ?" [11]

There is, nevertheless, in this preface one echo of the

[11] Allen, X, no. 2771. My translation.

earlier Erasmus. In discussing the ideal monk as one who, among other qualities, "has in his soul no conflicts of emotion warring among themselves or with God," he speaks of the possibility of being a monk, "even in the halls of princes, in public magistracies, and in the midst of commerce with men." Perhaps he was thinking of his friend Sir Thomas More who wore a hair shirt while serving as Lord Chancellor, but in any case he seems to be affirming that an inner asceticism and serenity are more important than the outward signs of the monk's cowl or even the dedication to a conventual life. On the whole, however, in spite of this one recurrence of an earlier theme, this preface shows an attitude toward monasticism very different from what might have been expected from the author of the *Praise of Folly* and some of the *Colloquies*. Coming from the pen of one who had himself fled from his monastery, rejecting the monastic discipline and spending years of his life in negotiations with ecclesiastical authority to regularize his position, these statements of his later years are the more remarkable. Erasmus now makes perfectly clear that his previous attacks had been directed against abuses and that he accepts the institution of monasticism as he accepts the body of doctrine which he now regards the reformers as having repudiated.

Another letter of these years indicates Erasmus's willingness to support the jurisdictional authority of the papacy. In the summer of 1533 a sympathetic young Portuguese friend, Damiao de Goes, had written to Erasmus to ask his opinion on the thorny legal and moral problems arising from the divorce of Henry VIII. Erasmus replied in a letter in which he summarized the legal issues involved, but pointed out that contrary to rumor, he had never taken a position on the issue of who was in the right.[12] He does, however, support the papal primacy and the authority of the pope to make the final decision. In the same letter he implied his approval of Damiao de Goes's appeal to the papacy in behalf of the Laplanders. These people were being subjected to depredations and were threatened with extinction by the advances of the Swedes on the Baltic. It was the identical issue that was currently being debated in the New World where Las Casas, the Spanish bishop, was trying to defend the rights of the Indians against the Aristotelian theories of natural slavery. Goes had considered that the pope was the appropriate authority to regulate the relations between the Christian and heathen and in directing his appeal to the papacy had turned to Erasmus for support. On these two causes, therefore, one involving a Christian ruler and the other the relation between Christian and non-Christian peoples, Erasmus indicates his acceptance of the traditional authority of the papacy.

The religious position indicated by these citations, is, however, most strongly confirmed by the extensive correspondence with Boniface Amerbach during the years of Erasmus's residence in Freiburg. Amerbach, who had held since 1524 the chair of civil law at Basel, was the closest of Erasmus's friends and his particular confidant in this period. To no one else did Erasmus speak with such frankness as to this jurist whose loving admiration for Erasmus was expressed not only in every one of the considerable number of letters he wrote to Erasmus but also

<hr>

[12] Allen, X, no. 2846.

in many of his letters to other correspondents. In their exchanges both men deplore the fact that Erasmus has had to leave Basel and both recognize that they must be cautious about the expression of their views. Again and again, Erasmus writes to Boniface Amerbach warning him that his words are for Boniface's eyes only. Again and again, also, they deplore the seditions and tumults which the Reformation had brought in its train. In a letter written shortly after his removal to Freiburg, Erasmus wrote to Boniface that the Reformers at Basel were destroying learning, that no students would come to Basel in the future unless they wished to be suspected of heresy. And he concluded by pointing out, that it would perhaps be more fitting for Boniface to teach Scythian law than Roman law. Again, he says that nothing can be written so prudently and circumspectly but that it may be taken out of its context and bring calumny on the author. Boniface writes despairingly from Basel that, "here we live under the pretext of the Evangel and there is nothing which the liberty of the Evangel does not now permit or order." There is much discussion of the possibility of Boniface leaving Basel, and Erasmus accuses him of being too considerate of his property in Basel and the interest of his family. When the ordinance was issued forcing the citizens of Basel to accept the interpretation of the eucharist by Oecolampadius, Boniface resisted and presented his case to the Senate. Writing to Erasmus about his difficulties, he said, "In the old days we used to consider that the pontiff was tyrannical but now that the evangelicals have power they call it liberty." The evangelical party was depriving the professors of immunities which had been theirs for many years. Boniface can imagine that he is really living at Constantinople under the arbitrary power of the Turk. His only hope is that if, formerly, one could be Christian under the heathen, perhaps also those who like himself have to live under the tyranny of the evangelical creed will be allowed to be Christian. The frankness of these exchanges, the confidence that Amerbach and Erasmus placed in each other, give all the more weight to the representation of their real views in these letters. Although some of the individual Catholic critics of Erasmus are not spared, nevertheless the position of Erasmus against the Reformation is made abundantly clear.[13]

If we turn from the correspondence to the literary activity of Erasmus in these last seven years of his life, we find confirmation of the religious position described and affirmed in the letters. Throughout this period Erasmus continued his great scholarly labors, producing many editions and commentaries. At the same time he composed several tracts for the times and works of devotion and carried on a continuing polemic with his critics and enemies. As he was more and more afflicted with arthritis and could at times hardly hold the pen, he relied to a greater extent than formerly on dictation to secretaries and as a result some of the works of this period have not the literary finish of earlier productions.

From Freiburg he sent to the Froben press at Basel his editions of the works of Aristotle, Demosthenes, and Livy.

[13] The letters referred to in this paragraph are Allen, VIII, nos, 2152, 2160, 2180, 2199, 2224, 2248.

Among the Church Fathers he devoted himself especially to the Greeks and edited or revised earlier editions of St. Basil, St. John Chrysostom, Gregory of Nazianzus, and, above all, Origen. It was, in fact, to see his edition of the works of the latter through the press that Erasmus returned to Basel in the summer of 1535. There he died in the following year, before the Origen was finished, and it was published shortly after his death with a preface by his great friend Beatus Rhenanus. There is a certain artistic completeness in the fact that his last scholarly labors should have been concerned with this Greek Father who had always especially attracted Erasmus and who had directly influenced certain of his formulations in his first major work, the *Enchiridion,* written in 1501. In spite of the fact that Origen is not the most orthodox of the Christian Fathers, there is nothing in Erasmus's edition of his works nor of those of the other Greek Fathers to which objection could be taken on doctrinal grounds without impugning the influence of these Fathers on the thought of the Western Church. Erasmus was not responsible for the historical fact of their influence and he was here simply pursuing what had long been his principal object, namely, the provision of better texts of both classic and Christian sources.

Of his own writing during the Freiburg years, the works which are most important from the point of view of doctrine are the *Vidua Christiana,* addressed to the sister of Charles V, Mary of Hungary, and written just before Erasmus's departure from Basel in 1529; the *Catechism* of 1533 together with the *De sarcienda ecclesiae concordia* of the same year; the *De preparatione ad mortem* of 1534 and finally the *De puritate tabernaculi* and the *Ecclesiastes* of 1536.[14]

The treatise on the Christian widow, which had been repeatedly requested from Erasmus by one of the advisors of Mary of Hungary, contains views on the subject of virginity, marriage, and widowhood that Erasmus had already earlier expressed. It has been argued that these views are in fact basically anti-Catholic, and that if we consider the implications of the Erasmian views on the sacrament of matrimony, it will be seen that Erasmus was in reality attacking the very foundation of the ecclesiastical tradition.[15] It seems more reasonable to conclude, however, that Erasmus was very genuinely convinced that there were divergencies in the views of the early authorities on this subject, as he says in the letter to Ber which has been quoted earlier.[16] It must also be said that, whatever other works of Erasmus were the subject of contemporary criticism, no voice was raised at the time against a treatise presented to so orthodox and highly placed a personage as the Emperor's sister.

Of the *Catechism* or *Explanatio Symboli apostolorum,* it has been generally held that, if the particular definitions of Erasmus are not always as complete as they might be, at least they do not deviate from orthodoxy. The distinctions drawn between heresy and error were perfectly in accord with the Roman tradition and they were extremely relevant in an age when the tone of religious controversy

[14] These treatises are collected in Erasmus, *Opera omnia,* J. LeClerc, ed., 10 vols. in 11 (Leyden, 1703–1706), vol. V.
[15] See Telle, *Erasme et le Septième Sacrament,* pp. 423–438.
[16] Allen, VIII, no. 2136.

had become so violent. It is significant that Luther in his *Table Talk* violently denounced this *Catechism*.[17]

The *De sarcienda* and the *De puritate tabernaculi* were expositions of Psalms to which Erasmus gave a topical application in the service of his by now traditional plea for peace and unity. The *De preparatione ad mortem* certainly contained an emphasis on the distinction between the spirit and the letter which Erasmus had taken from the Pauline Epistles and which runs through so many of his writings on Christian subjects. Although in this treatise he dwells again on the importance of an inward repentance and an inward serenity, there is nothing in his treatment of the efficacy of the sacraments which could be regarded as suspicious.

The *Ecclesiastes* is Erasmus's last work. It is a long treatise on preaching, its history and purposes in the Christian Church, the occasions on which it can be most effective, the rhetorical devices that the preacher may adopt, and the organization and classification of the sources of his subject matter. The fact that he took up this topic at the end of his life again confers on his literary career a certain artistic completeness. His first work had been the *Enchiridion,* which is a description of the essence of Christianity written for a layman living in the world; now more than thirty years later he wrote a manual of instruction for the discharge of one of the essential duties of those who held spiritual office.

In none of these works of the last years was the Council of Trent able to find objectionable material. The reaction against Erasmus had proceeded so far by the time of the

[17] Luther, *Tischreden* (Weimar, 1921), III, 3795; IV, 4899.

Index of Paul IV in 1559 that all the works of Erasmus were condemned without reservation including those the dedication of which had been accepted by previous popes. However, in the so-called *Tridentine Index* five years later there were explicitly prohibited only the *Folly,* the *Colloquies,* the *De Lingua*—a treatise on language and its powers for good and evil, written in 1525 and received with some favor by such Reformers as Oecolampadius—the *Institutio matrimonii,* the *de interdicto esu carnium,* and finally, an Italian translation of the *Paraphrase of St. Mathew.* In this document it is also declared that other works of Erasmus will be censored as long as they have not been reviewed and expurgated by the theological faculties of Louvain and Paris.[18] This is not the place to consider the later history of the attitude of the Church to Erasmus;[19] successive editions of the *Index* have varied in the comprehensiveness of their condemnation and in the most recent edition of the *Index librorum prohibitorum* the name of Erasmus is altogether removed. My point here is that even in the early discussions of those aspects of Erasmus's writing which were considered unorthodox, there were no explicit references to the works of the later period of his life.

In considering all the evidence of these years, I therefore come to the conclusion that Erasmus regarded himself as a Catholic Christian. I do not mean to deny the points which had divided him and still divided him from his Catholic opponents, particularly, Cardinal Aleander, the

[18] Fr. H. Reusch, *Die Indices Librorum Prohibitorum des Sechzehnten Jahrhunderts* (Tübingen, 1886), p. 185.
[19] See Andreas Flitner, *Erasmus in Urteil Seiner Nachwelt* (Tübingen, 1952).

monks of Spain, the theologians of Louvain, and Alberto Pio, Prince of Carpi. All these individuals and groups had seized items in Erasmus's earlier writing which they regarded as heretical or committing Erasmus to the Reformation. He struck out against them sometimes more convincingly, sometimes less convincingly. But in his less controversial moments, such as his letters to Amerbach and his last works he made perfectly clear that he had no intention of attacking the institutions or the doctrine of the Church. To attack abuses in the old dispensation was not the same thing as a transfer of allegiance to a new Church.

The late Augustin Renaudet, one of the greatest of modern students of Erasmus, has proposed the term "third Church" as a description of Erasmus's real religious allegiance in the later period of his life. This conception of the "third Church" is founded upon Erasmus's statement to Luther in the *First Hyperaspistes,* "I will support this Church, (i.e., Rome), until I see a better." [20] There is no indication that he ever saw a better in reality. In his mind's eye he could cherish an ideal in the light of which he could continue to correct abuses and to criticize aspects of Roman policy. This ideal meant, not that he labored to found a new Church, equidistant from Luther and from Rome, but that he hoped to correct at least some aspects of the Church to which he had given his allegiance. If he failed, if everything was not to his satisfaction, yet still Rome was the Church which he would continue to support.

[20] *Opera omnia,* X, 1258A. Cited in A. Renaudet, *Erasme et l'Italie* (Geneva, 1954), p. 175.

The existence of his hopes for modification raises the question whether the term "modernist" can appropriately be applied to the thought and action of Erasmus. If this terms means no more than that in Erasmus's philosophy and theology the intellectual interests of his age were reflected, then it may be accepted. It is in this sense that Gilson declared in an often-quoted aphorism that the "Modernism of St. Thomas Aquinas was the last which succeeded in the history of the Church." If, however, the term "modernism" is intended to carry with it implications derived from the history of the Church in the nineteenth and twentieth centuries and especially connotations of progressive revelation and symbolism, then it is unhistorical to apply it to the work of Erasmus.[21]

We cannot accurately describe the Catholic quality of the thought of Erasmus by applying to it categories derived from later historical experience whether of the twentieth century or so soon after Erasmus's death as the sessions of the Council of Trent. It must again and again be emphasized that on many points of doctrine there did not exist during Erasmus's lifetime the clarifications provided by the Tridentine definitions. We must not judge Erasmus's religion from a post-Tridentine point of view any more than we must judge that of St. Thomas More or Thomas à Kempis with both of whom Erasmus has great affinities. He was after all educated in the schools of the Brethren of the Common Life and the tradition that produced the *Imitation of Christ* contributed powerfully to the formation of Erasmus's conception of the

[21] For a discussion of this question see Bouyer, *Autour d'Erasme,* ch. xi.

essence of the Christian message. More was perhaps Erasmus's closest and most congenial friend for a long period and his learning, charity, and humor equally shaped the Erasmian ideals. These ideals may have nurtured hopes for changes in Rome; they did not look toward the formation of a new Church. In Erasmus's own eyes and in those of his closest friends and contemporaries, he remained unequivocally a Catholic Christian and separated himself decisively from the conclusions of the Reformation.

In turning from Erasmus the Christian to Erasmus the humanist, it must be said that his religious convictions have been thought ambiguous because of the ways in which he presented and defended them. His commitment to Christianity was conditioned by his commitment to humanism and the style of his discourse whether in scholarly exposition or the heat of controversy was profoundly shaped by the tradition of Italian humanism.

In this tradition dialogue occupied a central place not only as a valid method of education but also as the most likely means by which an opponent might be converted. The renewed popularity of the Platonic dialogues was one of the features of the intellectual scene even in the early Italian Renaissance. There had of course been dialogues throughout the medieval period and some of them are texts of great importance in the history of law, political theory, and philosophy. On the whole, however, the preferred method of exposition in a medieval university was the scholastic disputation. In the social atmosphere created in certain of the Italian urban centers it was perhaps natural that the Platonic dialogues should enjoy a re-

newed popularity. These conversations spoke more directly and seemed more natural to the members of a society
who daily met to hold conversations in the piazza or in
the congenial atmosphere of a Renaissance garden. The
famous chancellor of Florence, Coluccio Salutati, speaking
to his young visitors in Bruni's *Dialogus ad Petrum Histrum,* reminds them that "there is nothing more truly
educational than a disputation among friends." [22]

The emphasis on dialogue had certain obvious consequences for the conduct of intellectual arguments. In the
first place it exalted the art of persuasion. That character
in a dialogue who could use a persuasive rhetoric to make
his views prevail might come off better in the end than
another who confined himself to asserting what he believed to be the truth. In the second place, the views that
were really those of the author of the dialogue could be
concealed under the opinions attributed to one of the
characters. If the author were charged with unpopular
or even impermissible opinions which had been expressed
by one of the characters, he could always reply that these
were not his opinions at all but that they had been introduced and put into the mouth of the character in the
dialogue in order to be refuted.

Both these characteristics—the emphasis on the art of
persuasion and the concealment of the author's true
opinions by resort to dramatization—are abundantly to
be seen in the work of Erasmus. We think at once of the
Colloquies, those fictitious conversations which began as

---

[22] Leonardo Bruni, *Ad Petrum Paulum Histrum Dialogus,* as edited
and translated by E. Garin, in *Prosatori Latini del Quattrocento* (Milan,
1952), pp. 48–51.

pedagogical devices but grew into dramatic exchanges involving all the debated issues of politics and religion of Erasmus's generation. In a larger sense, however, the characteristics of dialogue were part of the whole style of Erasmus. Aside from the many of his works which are cast in the dialogue form, almost all his writing partakes of a conversational tone and follows forms of rhetorical persuasion. What is the whole vast collection of letters, perhaps the greatest single source for the intellectual history of his age, but a continuing dialogue with his contemporaries?

A. N. Whitehead, in his *Adventures of Ideas,* has brilliantly illustrated the difference created between different epochs by changes of tone in the way in which controversy is conducted. We cannot transpose the style of Socrates in dealing with his opponents to the age of St. Augustine; "Can we imagine Augustine urbanely approaching Pelagius with 'a suggestion of ours respecting the nature of grace?'" [23] The Renaissance was an age of persuasion and Erasmus epitomized his time. Long before the period of his old age which has concerned us here, Erasmus had publicly urged the value of considering opposing opinions and cited many of the intellectual and critical battles of antiquity. In the summer of 1504 he found in a monastery near Louvain a manuscript of the *Annotations on the New Testament* of Lorenzo Valla. He published this important work and, in the preface that he wrote to the Paris edition, he confessed that so far from being a vice, he considered a difference of opinion among authors to be a virtue. The friend who applauds is not

[23] A. N. Whitehead, *Adventures of Ideas* (New York, 1933), p. 135.

more welcome than the enemy who criticizes. If the criticism is true Erasmus leaves the encounter more learned, if it is false, he becomes at least more attentive and cautious and in the end a more zealous defender of the truth.[24] But the important proviso was added *ne in rabiem exeat ac citra convicia consistat,* that the controversy not fall into raging and wrangling.

In the letter to Bucer already quoted he declares: "It was my intention to correct any matters affected by superstition little by little and more by persuasion than by force."[25] Here Erasmus voices the ideals of humanist discourse. It was not the tradition of the Reformation or that of the Council of Trent. This Erasmus discovered in his encounters with Luther and with Aleander, for both of whom it was more important to assert the truth than it was to seek to persuade. Erasmus's own sense of the failure of his style of discourse marks the change from one age to another.

There is another aspect of this change which is perhaps even more fundamental than the transition from persuasion to dogmatic assertion. It is one of the characteristics of successful dialogue that the participating characters speak at least to some extent a common language and are willing to hear the opposing arguments without breaking into an outburst of temper. The participants cannot be too incompatible and personal differences must be smoothed over in the interest of harmonious exchange. The effort to maintain this kind of dialogue in the larger sense perhaps explains why in reading the works of Erasmus we have so often the feeling that what is personal and inti-

[24] Allen, I, no. 182.
[25] Allen, IX, no. 2615. My translation.

mate is kept at a distance. Many students of Erasmus's character have felt that he mistrusted the expression of deep emotion. The letters he wrote on the receipt of the most grevious news such as the execution of Berquin in Paris in 1529 and More in England in 1535 do not seem to express a cry from the heart.[26] Consider also for example his letter of consolation to Boniface Amerbach on the death of his three-year-old daughter. "A man who is a jurisconsult and has counselled others to obey the laws of Caesar must himself obey the laws of nature which lead those who are willing but compel those who are not."[27] Although Boniface professed the deep satisfactions that he derived from the consolations of Erasmus, the modern reader may be inclined to feel that the tone leaves something to be desired in expressing comfort from one intimate friend to another in such a situation. Of course it may be said, and with truth, that the Latin language itself imposed a degree of formality, and that the personality of the writer could never be vividly expressed in phrases which had been so self-consciously revived from the Latin authors of antiquity. Yet it is quite possible that this very artificiality was congenial to Erasmus; the fact that he could always keep his deepest personal feelings at a distance may explain his life-long devotion to writing in Latin. Few others carried so far their dedication to the cause of Latinity and it is significant that Erasmus's great contemporaries and near contemporaries such as Luther, Calvin, Rabelais, and Montaigne felt that they had to express themselves in the vernacular.

Both the form of the dialogue and the use of Latin may

[26] Allen, VIII, no. 2188; XI, no. 3036.
[27] Allen, X, no. 2678. My translation.

thus be seen as a form of Renaissance "style" which was particularly congenial to Erasmus. Although we have been accustomed since the time of Burckhardt to debate "individualism" as a characteristic of the Renaissance, might it not be suggested that in reality large sectors of Renaissance thought are more characterized by a concern for the ideal type than for the individual? The prince, the courtier, the gentleman, the ideal scholar are all familiar subjects of Renaissance speculation and, although the *Colloquies* of Erasmus are filled with vivid details about an abbot, an innkeeper, a soldier, a butcher, a fishmonger, yet they speak as types and not with the dimension of emotional reality conveyed by Luther when he was arguing against the ideas of Erasmus in the *De servo arbitrio*. From this point of view it is possible to maintain that when we move from the Renaissance to the Reformation we move not only from a realm of discourse in which persuasion was regarded as more important than dogmatic assertion, but also from a world of ideal types to a world in which the individual with all his idiosyncrasies was more realistically recognized. Erasmus saw many signs of this change in his later years. As he struggled to keep the dialogue open, to maintain the kind of disputation of which he had spoken in the introduction to the edition of Valla, he was involved in an increasing number of controversies many of which were deplored by his friends as unworthy of his attention.

One such controversy, in itself of small scope, nevertheless brings vividly before us the changes in Erasmus's thinking about himself and his work in the last decade of his life. Just before his removal from Basel to Freiburg, a Spanish friend, Alfonso Valdes, had written to him reporting that certain of his enemies among the Spanish monks were attacking Erasmus's device as an example of intolerable arrogance. This device was a representation of the Roman boundary god Terminus with the motto *concedo nulli,* "I yield to none." Erasmus had found it on an antique gem that had been presented to him by a grateful pupil in Rome many years before, and ever since had used it as his emblem and official seal. It had been engraved by Holbein and carved by Metsys on the back of a medal representing Erasmus. Replying to his unfriendly critics, Erasmus pointed out how he had come by the device and recalled that in classical mythology Terminus, the sacred protector of boundaries, was the only god who had not yielded to Jupiter when the Temple of Jupiter was being built on the Capitoline hill in Rome. Hence the representation of the boundary god came to stand for the limit or end which could not be passed. Erasmus now says that he had come to think of the Terminus as symbolizing the end of life, that is, death, and that the motto, "I yield to none," far from being an arrogant statement by Erasmus on his own unlimited powers, is in fact regarded as spoken by Death whom no man can escape and who in fact puts an end to all human achievement. Thus the motto instead of an over-confident assertion of man's capacities, is in reality, a confession of man's fate.[28]

These protestations by Erasmus did not convince his enemies at the time and among modern scholars the view

---

[28] For a more extended discussion of this point, see M. P. Gilmore, "Erasmus: The Scholar and the World," in *Henry Wells Lawrence Memorial Lectures,* IV (New London, 1959), 27–43.

ER · ROT

TERMINVS

Corporis effigiem si quis non uidit Erasmi,
Hanc scitè ad uiuum picta tabella dabit.

has been put forward that Erasmus believed one thing in 1509, when he adopted the device, and another in 1528, when the Reformation had caused the hopes of his earlier period to fade into disillusionment.[29] However we may characterize the earlier years, when Erasmus more than once expressed himself as having lived to see the dawn of a golden age, there is no doubt that the letter in which he explained his device to his Spanish friend underlines the pessimism with which he now regarded the future. His health was feeble; many of his closest friends had died; he could no longer so confidently believe in the success of the causes he had most at heart; and the evil consequences of the religious dissensions seemed to him to reach a climax in the excesses of the siege of Munster in 1534 and the executions of More and Fisher in England.

By the time the latter news reached him at the end of August 1535 he was again in Basel. He had grown restless in Freiburg and thought of settling in Besançon where he was pressingly invited by the Senate and where he could be sure of a supply of the good wine of Burgundy that he felt was necessary to his health. Another alternative was Antwerp where he had old associations and would be hospitably received by the Regent Mary of Hungary. Without committing himself definitely to either solution, he decided to go temporarily to Basel to see through the press the *Ecclesiastes* and the edition of *Origen*. There he was received with great warmth by his old friends and installed in a house belonging to Froben. Gradually it became clear that his physical condition did not permit

---

[29] See E. Wind, *Journal of the Warburg Institute* 1:66–69 (1937–1938).

any further change of residence. He had six years earlier proclaimed that he could not live in a city which was officially under the dispensation of the Reform but it was his fate to spend his last months there. In the spring of 1536 he grew rapidly weaker and died on July 12, 1536. Although there has been much discussion of the question whether Erasmus was attended by a Catholic priest in his last moments, it appears that his secretary, Lambert Coomans, who was afterwards a priest and dean of the chapter of the Cathedral of Turnhout, was not in orders at the time he was in Erasmus's service and, therefore, as a priest, could not have administered the last rites.[30]

By his will, which he had taken the precaution to have authenticated by the Emperor, the papacy, and the town council of Basel, lest there be any difficulties created because of his illegitimate birth or because of conflicting claims of jurisdiction, he appointed Boniface Amerbach his heir and Jerome Froben and Nicholas Episcopius his executors.[31] Boniface Amerbach wrote, in a preface addressed to John Paungartner, a brief and moving description of Erasmus's funeral.[32] The body was borne to the cathedral by the students of the university and attended by all the professors and magistrates. When the monument was erected, which can still be seen with its inscription celebrating to posterity the learning and virtue of Erasmus, Amerbach caused the Terminus to be represented upon it.

[30] See the discussion of this question in V. de Caprariis, "Qualche precisazione sulla morte di Erasmo," *Revista Storica Italiana* 43:100–108 (1951), and the literature therein cited.
[31] Allen, XI, appendix 25, pp. 362–365.
[32] Allen, XII, no. 3141.

FRANCESCO PETRARCA

LORENZO VALLA

ANDREA ALCIATO

FILIPPO DECIO

JACQUES CUJAS

BARTOLUS OF SASSOFERRATO

GUILLAUME BUDE

GIASONE DEL MAINO

Thus was buried in a Protestant city and by a Protestant minister this Catholic whose works were to be condemned by the Council of Trent, this revolutionary who had become a conservative. Erasmus, too often, has been described as a neutral who preferred to remain above the battle and who was temperamentally incapable of taking a stand. The consideration of the thought and action especially of his later years shows that he had convictions on which, to use the language of his ambiguous motto, he did not yield. One of them was his conviction as a Christian. This led him to reject the Reformation and to support what was best and endure what was worst (the verb *fero* which he used in the famous sentence to Luther covers both senses) in the Church for which his friend More suffered martyrdom. A second was his conviction as a humanist. This led him to maintain that even the deepest commitments should be defended and advanced by persuasion rather than by force. These two convictions dominated the last decades of the life of Erasmus and their coexistence makes clear the fact that his greatest intellectual and moral significance lies not in the fact that he refused to take sides, but that in taking sides he refused to regard the dialogue as ended.

VI

BONIFACE AMERBACH

ERASMUS once wrote to Boniface Amerbach, "you are a tame domestic animal." [1] From one point of view there is indeed an atmosphere of domesticity about Amerbach's life. He was a dutiful son, a loving husband and father, a loyal friend, and a patriotic citizen. The qualities of filial piety, family affection, and civic pride are conspicuous virtues at any time, but we may agree with Erasmus that they seem to take on an even more domestic character in an age when public issues became ever more compelling and Europe was echoing to the battle cries of the Reformation. Yet, from another point of view, the citizen of Basel in its golden age was the observer and critic of the mind of European Christendom; there is hardly any aspect of the intellectual history of his generation untouched in the correspondence so constantly exchanged between the house in Basel and the scholars and men of letters of most of the countries of western Europe. Although the course of his physical life was domestic and circumscribed, his intellectual horizon was ecumenical.

In every revolutionary period there are individuals—sometimes in surprisingly large numbers—who are able to lead quiet and ordered lives. Subsequent generations

[1] P. S. Allen, ed., *Opus Epistolarum Des. Erasmi Roterodami,* 12 vols. (Oxford, 1906–1958), X, no. 2642. My translation.

may think first of scenes of violence and disorder—the
storming of the city hall, the destruction of the images—
but in fact many men were able to go about the business
of getting an education, practicing a profession, founding
a family, and accumulating property, in accordance with
the stable traditions of the society into which they were
born. In the opinions of such men we may sometimes find
a more sensitive barometer of the nature and significance
of ideological changes than in the thought of those who
fought in the front line of the battle or who penned the
manifestoes of revolution.

Boniface Amerbach was not of the stuff of which heroes
and martyrs are made. Yet sensitive, idealistic, and intel-
lectually curious as he was, he could not avoid making
judgments on the issues created first by the dissemination
of Italian Renaissance scholarship and second by the
challenge of Luther's criticism. To his trusted friends,
especially his teachers Zasius in Germany and Alciato in
Italy and his former fellow pupils Montaigne, the French
lawyer, and Lopis, the Spanish doctor, and above all to
his admired Erasmus, he spoke freely and at length, giving
us a chronicle of the intellectual history of his generation
rivalled only by the correspondence of Erasmus himself.
Yet, these were private expressions of opinion and, as the
situation became more critical, there is increasing reference in his letters to the necessity for circumspection, to
the danger of persecution, to the loss of those bright
hopes which Boniface and his friends had entertained
in 1517 and 1518 when it had been possible to regard
Erasmus and Luther as the inaugurators of a new golden
age. At least twice, however, Boniface Amerbach felt

compelled to take a public stand. The first of these incidents concerned his professional life and was occasioned
by the assumption of the professorship of law at the
University of Basel in 1525. The second concerned his
religious opinions and was occasioned by the adoption
of the Reformation in Basel in 1529 with the consequent
pressure for conformity. Both these episodes in the intellectual life of Amerbach have been the subject of careful
monographs[2] and it is not the purpose of this essay to
consider in detail either Amerbach's views on the teaching
of law or his religious opinions. On the other hand, the
presuppositions which he brought to both these problems
and his solutions may be usefully studied as a contribution
not only to our knowledge of Amerbach's character and
personality but also to our understanding of the problem
of the relation of the individual to inherited intellectual
tradition in an age of revolution.

Boniface Amerbach was born in Basel on October 11,
1495, the third son of a well-known printer Johannes or
Hans Amerbach.[3] The latter had established his press in

[2] On the law, see Guido Kisch, *Humanismus und Jurisprudenz:
Der Kampf zwischen mos italicus und mos gallicus an der Universität
Basel*, Basler Studien zur Rechtswissenschaft, vol. 42 (Basel, 1955).
See also by Kisch, vols. 34, 54, and 56 in the same series: *Johannes
Sichardus als Basler Rechthistoriker* (Basel, 1952); *Bartolus und Basel*
(Basel, 1960); and, most recently, *Erasmus und die Jurisprudenz seiner
Zeit: Studien zum humanistischen Rechtsdenken* (Basel, 1960). On the
religious issue see Theodor Burckhardt-Biedermann, *Bonifacius Amer-
bach und die Reformation* (Basel, 1894).
[3] The basic published sources on Amerbach's life are contained in
Die Amerbachkorrespondenz, Alfred Hartmann, ed. (Basel, 1942–
1958). The 5 volumes so far published cover the years from 1481–1543.
Brief summaries of the principal dates of Boniface's life are given in

BONIFACE AMERBACH

Basel in 1475 and entered into partnership with Froben in 1500.[4] The partners were enthusiastic supporters of the highest ideals of humanist scholarship and in particular fostered the publication of the Church Fathers. Their work brought them into close connection with some of the greatest scholars of the age. To their hospitable house came men learned in Latin, Greek, and Hebrew, to participate in the great work of making available the basic texts of the Christian tradition. Chief among these scholars was Erasmus who was already embarked on his edition of the New Testament and the works of St. Jerome. The favoring environment and the privileged connection of their father with the learned world of Europe were undoubtedly the most decisive influences in the formation of the character and interests of Amerbach's sons.

Johannes Amerbach was determined that his children should have the best education that could be provided in the classical languages and that they should afterwards be trained for the professions of theology or law. In accordance with this plan the olders brothers had been sent to Freiburg and to Paris. Boniface began his education in the Engental near Basel as the private pupil of his father's friend Conrad Leontorius, a Cistercian monk, who had himself been a friend and pupil of the leading German humanists. He was learned in Greek, Latin, and Hebrew, and had himself contributed to the scholarly work of the Amerbach press.[5] Boniface spent only a few months with

---

Allen, II, no. 408, and Kisch, *Erasmus,* p. 344n, with references to the biographical literature.

[4] Allen, II, no. 309n.

[5] Hartmann, I, no. 18n.

this preceptor who nevertheless acquired sufficient knowledge of his pupil's capacities to send a wise and indulgent report to the elder Amerbach. The latter had expressed some impatience with Boniface's progress and Leontorius replied in a communication which breathes the spirit exemplified in the best humanist educators, "It is not the nature of man to be compelled but rather gradually and benevolently prompted." He begs the father not to marvel if he does not see a sudden change, "for with time natural abilities will flourish and mature." [6] These were sentiments which were to have a greater application to at least some aspects of Boniface's life than either his teacher or his father could have imagined.

After the short period under the direction of Leontorius, Boniface was sent to Schlettstadt where there was a school of increasing reputation in which his brothers had already preceded him. The school had been founded about the middle of the preceding century by a friend and contemporary of Hegius, the teacher of Erasmus, and its curriculum accordingly continued to reflect some of the characteristic intellectual and spiritual interests associated with the Brethren of the Common Life. Here under Gebweiler he followed a course of study which, although it showed some influence from the centers of learning in Italy, still retained much of the traditional instruction. [7] In 1509 he returned to Basel and enrolled in the university of his native city. At the same time he had the unusual opportunity of pursuing Greek and Hebrew studies with the distinguished scholars who had come to Basel to

[6] Hartmann, I, no. 336. My translation.
[7] D. A. Fechter, "Bonifacius Amerbach," *Beiträge zur Vaterlandischen Geschichte*, II (Basel, 1843), 176–177.

collaborate on the edition of St. Jerome undertaken by the Amerbach press and who had received the hospitality of the Amerbach household.[8]

Boniface became master of arts at the University of Basel on January 9, 1513, and determined to go next to Freiburg to continue his education in the law with Ulrich Zasius. Zasius was already establishing his reputation as one of the great masters of jurisprudence, sharing with Alciato in Italy and Budé in France the credit for the new conquests in the study of the Roman law. He received Boniface into his house in Freiburg and thus began a relationship which came more to resemble that of father and son than that of master and pupil. Until the death of Zasius in 1535 there was maintained a correspondence that religious differences were never able to impair and which is a tribute to the degree of affection and good will on both sides.[9]

During his stay in Freiburg Boniface returned to Basel at the beginning of 1514, on the occasion of his father's death, and there had the opportunity for the first time of meeting Erasmus. The great scholar was then at the height of the literary fame that had followed the publication of the *Adages* and the *Moriae Encomium*. Perhaps on his side Erasmus needed the warmth, the admiration, the encouragement which he received from the younger

[8] *Ibid.*, pp. 178–182.
[9] See, on the relations between them, R. Stintzing, *Ulrich Zasius: Ein Beitrag zur Geschichte der Rechtswissenschaft im Zeitalter der Reformation* (Basel, 1857), *passim,* and Alfred Hartmann, "Familäres aus der Amerbachkorrespondenz," *Basler Jahrbuch* (1951), pp. 35–57. The older collection of Zasius' letters, *Epistolae ad viros aetatis suae doctissimos,* J. A. Riegger, ed. (Ulm, 1774), includes valuable prefatory material, although the letters exchanged between Zasius and Amerbach are included in Hartmann.

Huldrichus Zasius / der Rechten
Doctor zu Freyburg.   mort. 1535.

scholar in the fullest measure. And perhaps on his side Boniface was at the moment of his father's death in search of an authority whom he could fully respect, who could give him counsel on problems of intellectual and spiritual direction. Whatever the motivation, there began in these months a friendship which was of critical importance in the lives of both. Although they later differed in some of their reactions to the public events which they experienced and particularly to the coming of the Reformation to Basel, there was no individual in whose judgment Erasmus came to feel so much confidence, and when he died in 1536 it was Amerbach who was named his heir and executor of the trust funds established under his will.[10]

For five more years Boniface continued his studies with Zasius at Freiburg but then returned to Basel where he continued the pursuit of his historical and philological interests in the circle of scholars gathered around the Froben press. In May of 1520 he went to Avignon to study with Alciato and, with one interruption when he had to leave the city because of the plague, he continued there until 1524. In August of that year he was, through the influence of Zasius, offered a lectureship at Freiburg. Before he was able to begin his duties at this university, however, he was proposed for the professorship of civil law at Basel.[11] In order to be qualified for the latter posi-

[10] On Erasmus's legacy, Carl Roth, "Das Legatum Erasmianum" *Gedenkschrift zum 400 Todestage des Erasmus von Rotterdam* (Basel, 1936), pp. 282–298, and Alfred Hartmann, "Bonifacius Amerbach als Verwalter der Erasmus-stiftung," *Basler Jahrbuch* (1957), pp. 7–28. The text of the will is printed in Allen, XI, appendix 25.

[11] Kisch, *Humanismus und Jurisprudenz,* pp. 37, 134–135.

tion it was necessary that he take his doctor's degree in the civil law and for this purpose he returned to Avignon in February 1525. He, thus, received his final law degree twelve years after taking his master's degree at Basel. In an age when the doctorate in law or theology was generally supposed to take five to seven years this was regarded even by his friends as excessive. It was a comment on his character that Boniface was considered in danger of becoming a perpetual student and, perhaps, this may have been a family failing, as in later years Boniface's own son Basil was with difficulty persuaded to bring to an end his pleasant, if unduly prolonged, career as a student in the leading universities of Europe.[12]

At the time of his return to Basel Boniface found the new methods of teaching the law already established in what he regarded as an exaggerated form. Although he himself had received his legal education under two of the greatest masters of the renaissance of legal studies, he now began to perceive that the humanist principles of exegesis could be carried too far. The great revolution in legal studies, as in other branches of knowledge, had centered on an attempt to achieve a direct understanding of the meaning of the sources through the application of grammatical and philological analysis. In philosophy, theology, and law Petrarch and his followers had appealed over the heads of the medieval commentators to the authors of the basic texts. In the fifteenth century the great names of Lorenzo Valla and Angelo Poliziano are associated with the development of the attack on glossators and post-glossators alike. The first in his *De insigniis et armis*

---

[12] Burckhardt-Biedermann, pp. 117–120.

delivered his influential indictment of Bartolus while the second planned the critical edition of the Florentine codex of the Pandects.[13]

Many of the principles of the humanist critique had been received and applied by the great school of jurisprudence at the beginning of the sixteenth century. Alciato and Zasius were, however, never as extreme in their condemnation of the post-glossators as some of their humanist predecessors. Alciato specifically recognized the legal acuity of the medieval commentators and conceded that if they wrote bad Latin this was to be attributed to the fault of the age and not to the men themselves. Although he often wrote a barbarous language Bartolus was a master of legal science.[14]

These views were even more forcefully expressed by Amerbach when he returned to Basel in 1524 and found established in the university a kind of teaching which represented to him the pedantry of the grammarian who was completely ignorant of the history of the law. While he was still considering the lectureship offered at Freiburg, and before he had committed himself to the chair at Basel, he reported to his friends on his reaction to the lectures which were being given on the civil law at Basel by one Johannes Sichard, the successor of Cantiuncula.[15] To his fellow pupil at Avignon he wrote as follows, speaking of his own doubts about his capacity to undertake the lectureship at Freiburg:

---

[13] The most recent account of the school of humanist jurisprudence is D. Maffei, *Gli inizi dell'umanesimo giuridico* (Milan, 1956).

[14] *Ibid.*, p. 52.

[15] See Kisch, *Johannes Sichardus.*

I see many around me who do not fear to undertake such a task, although they have hardly opened the *Pandects* and scarcely know the names of the various problems they are expected to elucidate. We have such a one at Basel now, the successor of our Claudius (Cantiuncula), a man who, although he is not unlearned in the Latin language, is nevertheless completely unskilled in legal science which he never practiced. He undertakes the interpretation of the *Pandects* as if he were explaining a comedy of Terence or Plautus with all the glosses and interpreters cast aside . . . I remember that the day after I had returned to Basel, having heard the fame of this man bruited abroad, I went to hear him but I heard nothing but grammatical interpretations with an immoderate polemic against the doctors and glossators at whose work he had never looked.[16]

The letter continues with a denunciation of the lecturer's boldness in defending himself as an expert in legal studies and reflections on how easy it is for people to parrot words which they do not understand. Driven by hunger, men will do anything for money. This severe condemnation Boniface repeated in much the same terms to his former professor Alciato who had by this time returned to Italy.[17]

Shortly after thus expressing himself to his friends Boniface gave more formal expression of his opinions in a *Defensio interpretum iuris civilis* originally perhaps intended as a discourse for the opening of the Freiburg lectures but reworked and delivered in the spring or summer of 1525 on the occasion of the beginning of his professorship at Basel.[18]

[16] Hartmann, II, no. 962. My translation.
[17] Hartmann, II, no. 963.
[18] The text of the *Defensio* is in Hartmann, III, 554–564, with an

In this discourse Boniface maintains that there has arisen a new race of men "selling themselves" under the name of jurisconsults. These false representatives of legal studies repudiate Bartolus and the other post-glossators as well as Accursius and the authors of the gloss. They, also, even go so far as to condemn the great figures of Roman jurisprudence in the interest of recovering the most ancient sources of the law. Boniface freely admits that there are in the law a great many opinions and a great variety of meanings. Yet he does not see what there is to condemn in this situation. The student will be more helped than hindered by considering the multiplicity of opinions. In comparison and analysis the way lies open for arriving at the truth. In this Boniface considers that the law does not differ from other studies in which the examination of many opinions gives an opportunity of probing more deeply and producing a more accurate conclusion.

These views in defense of the medieval commentators were perhaps, in part, inspired by Boniface's teacher, Alciato, who had defended Bartolus.[19] However, the particular combination of the *mos italicus* or emphasis upon the application of the rules of law to contemporary conditions with the *mos gallicus* or emphasis on historical understanding of the legal texts was a product of Boniface's own experience and reflection. The importance of this synthesis in the University of Basel and in the develop-

---

introductory note on the various versions. See also Kisch, *Humanismus und Jurisprudenz,* pp. 79–97.

[19] Maffei, *Gli inizi dell'umanesimo giuridico,* p. 52; also P. E. Viard, *André Alciat, 1492–1550* (Paris, 1926), pp. 115 ff.

ment of Swiss jurisprudence has been brilliantly elucidated by Professor Kisch.[20]

There is one part of Boniface's argument, however, that can be more specifically connected with the humanist tradition of which he was in so many ways a conspicuous representative. This is the proposition that truth is the product of the consideration of the variety of opinions. The humanists had turned away from the rigidities of the medieval *sic et non* and from the formal development of an argument through a series of contradictory propositions. For Petrarch and his followers dialogue replaced dialectic as the most profitable method of discussion. In a conversational exchange it was possible to examine not only the formal contradiction but the whole spectrum of possibilities, the variety of opinions which might in the end contribute to the emergence of the truth. Among the early Italian humanists Salutati is particularly eloquent on the value of dialogue[21] and it is no accident that so much of humanist literature from Petrarch to Erasmus, whether embodied in formal dialogues or in epistolary exchanges, has the character of a conversation between individuals.[22] Boniface's admired Erasmus had declared how much he owed to discussions of this kind, even when the participants in the dialogue held opposing views, and his *Colloquies* were a brilliant example of the application of the method.[23] In the light of these characteristics of the general

[20] Kisch, *Humanismus und Jurisprudenz* and *Bartolus und Basel.*

[21] For Salutati, on the value of discussion, see Leonardo Bruni, *Ad Petrum Paulum Histrum Dialogus,* as edited and translated by E. Garin, in *Prosatori Latini del Quattrocento* (Milan, 1952), pp. 44–99.

[22] E. Garin, "La Storia del pensiero del rinascimento," *Medioevo e Rinascimento* (Bari, 1954), pp. 192–210.

[23] Allen, I, no. 182.

style of humanist discourse, it is possible to maintain that Boniface in developing his argument on truth elicited *ex opinionum varietate* was uttering a commonplace of the intellectual tradition in which he had been educated. It is also possible, however, that when he formulated his *defensio* he had more particularly in mind a work which had recently been published in Basel and in which the value of considering differing opinions was joined to a defense of Bartolus.

In 1518 Cratander's press in Basel published a slim volume containing three treatises by Lorenzo Valla. This collection, consisting of *De libera arbitrio, Apologia adversus calumniatores,* and *De insigniis et armis* had been assembled and published in Vienna two years before by Vadian (Joachim von Watt), at that time professor of poetry and eloquence at Maximilian's university, soon to be the reformer of St. Gall.[24] Vadian contributed a preface addressed to Victor Camp, doctor of laws, in which he describes how he had acquired these works of Valla from a canon of Wratislaw returning to Poland from Italy, and why he feels justified in publishing them. Although he recognizes that Valla is an opinionated and intemperate writer, he feels that the treatises will be valued especially by those who, like his friend, realize that the truth is not to be sought in one author alone "sed iudiciorum varietate." In discussing in particular the inclusion in the collection of Valla's treatise against Bartolus, Vadian makes clear his sense of shock that anyone should dare attack Bartolus who is known by all to be a man of genius.

---

[24] On Vadian, see Werner Näf, *Vadian und seine Stadt St. Gallen,* 2 vols. (St. Gall, 1944).

In spite of this he has been particularly glad to include this treatise because it will test the sincerity of the reader and his capacity to appreciate an argument against a generally received proposition. He recognizes that Valla is wrong in attacking Bartolus for his barbarous Latinity; it is the age and not the man who is responsible and, if Bartolus had lived in the time of Valla, Vadian is convinced that he would have fought the battle for an elegant Latinity as well as Valla himself.[25]

This little preface, composed by Vadian in Vienna in 1516 and republished by Cratander in Basel in 1518, thus contains two of the central propositions of Boniface Amerbach's *Defensio* of 1525, namely, the belief in the value of considering a variety of opinions as a means of arriving at the truth and the defense of Bartolus and the other medieval commentators.

[25] There exists in the Houghton Library at Harvard a copy of this edition on the title page of which is written in what appears to be the hand of Capito the following inscription: "Hunc libellum Dno Joan Fabro Iureconsulto litteratissimo vicario Reverendissimi Domini Constantiensis in spiritualibus et Domino observando V. Fa Capito dono mittet sitque felicem exoptans vitae cursum et ad ipsum amorem mutuum 7 Kal. Januarii 1518." From this we see that this copy just off Cratander's press was presented on the day after Christmas by Wolfgang Capito to Joannes Faber. Within a few years after this testimony to their mutual friendship and love, Capito and Faber had become bitter enemies over the issues of the Reformation. Faber (1478–1541) later became minister to King Ferdinand and Bishop of Vienna (see Allen, II, no. 386). Capito went from Basel where he had been dean and rector of the university to be the chancellor of Albert of Mainz whom in turn he left to become one of the Reformers of Strasbourg (Allen, II, no. 459). It is in retrospect ironic that a book dedicated to the value of considering opposing views and to the proposition that truth was to be elicited from a variety of judgments should have been the subject of an exchange between the two men who were soon to become such bitter enemies.

The second and far more difficult occasion on which Boniface Amerbach had to defend his views in public was a result of the coming of the Reformation. It was in the spring of 1518 while he was still a student in the house of Zasius that he encountered Luther's *Theses* for the first time and he and his roommate Thomas Blarer later recalled the enthusiasm with which they had pored over this manifesto.[26] This reaction was sustained in the immediately following period and during the debate of Luther with Eck, and the circulation of Luther's treatises of 1520, Boniface continued to believe that a golden age was dawning. Languages, medicine, and law had been restored. Now Erasmus and Luther were working together for the restoration of theology.[27] In 1520, during his first stay in Avignon, Boniface wrote to his brother that although there were diverse views of Luther yet the truth was at last showing itself.[28] After his temporary return to Basel in 1521 because of the plague in Avignon he sent to Alciato in Italy an account of the Diet of Worms which is almost wholly favorable to Luther. He wrote that no one had prevailed against Luther by rational arguments but only by force and authority.[29]

Within a short time, however, these earlier hopeful views began to be modified. During his second residence in Avignon and particularly in conversation with such men as Sadoleto, Boniface had the opportunity to see the extent of the divergent judgments on what Luther was accomplishing and the direction in which his reform was moving. In the last months of his residence at Avignon

[26] Burckhardt-Biedermann, pp. 1–3.
[27] Hartmann, II, no. 686.
[28] Hartmann, II, no. 747.
[29] Hartmann, II, no. 791.

he wrote to his brother expressing his amazement and horror at the social consequences of the application of some of the doctrines of the Reform, particularly the expropriation of monastic property and the violent termination of legal contracts which Boniface, as the result of both temperament and training, considered to be at the very foundation of the existence of human society.[30] A little later he complained about the attacks on Erasmus who, he considered, was the man who had done more than all others to improve the state of theology.[31] To his friend Montaigne in France he expressed his fears about the course of events in Germany.[32] In this letter he deplores increasingly radical measures such as the marriage of priests, monks, and nuns, and the secularization of ecclesiastical property, and here he begins to raise doubts about the biblicism of the Reformers and their neglect of the councils and the tradition of the Church.

Upon the beginning of his professorship in Basel he was asked by the council in the autumn of 1525 to serve on a commission to examine the orthodoxy of the treatise written by Oecolampadius *De genuina verborum domini "Hoc est corpus meum" expositione*. Besides Amerbach there were appointed to the commission Erasmus, Ber, and Cantiuncula.[33] Boniface petitioned the council to excuse him on the ground that he was a professor of civil law and not a theologian.[34] The council charged him with translating into German certain passages in the treatise of Oecolampadius which had been indicated by

[30] Hartmann, II, no. 928.
[31] Hartmann, II, no. 948.
[32] Hartmann, II, no. 956.
[33] Burckhardt-Biedermann, pp. 43–47.
[34] Hartmann, III, no. 1066.

Ber. When Boniface appealed to his old friend and teacher Zasius the latter denounced the work of Oecolampadius and made clear his rejection of the Reformation.[35] Boniface in a second communication to the council translated the passages which had been indicated, including the exposition of the figurative sense of the word *corpus* and the council rejected the treatise.[36]

During this controversy Boniface had been torn between his earlier admiration for Luther and his increasing apprehension of the effects of the Reformation. The doubts and hesitations and ultimately the rejection of the reform by his admired teachers and friends such as Zasius, Alciato, and Montaigne naturally caused him to take a more neutral, if not more actively hostile, attitude toward the further progress of the Reform in Basel. In the controversy between Erasmus and Luther on the freedom of the will, he remained loyal to his friend, and he felt that the attacks to which Erasmus was subjected by Luther and his supporters were motivated by hatred and envy.[37]

The uneasy condition of equilibrium between the old and the new confessions which existed in Basel during these years came to an end in the latter months of 1528 and the beginning of 1529. The council had been composed in part of Catholics in the period when Boniface had been asked to serve on the examining commission on the doctrine of Oecolampadius, and the priests or pastors of the various churches had liberty to conduct worship in accordance with their convictions. There was,

[35] Hartmann, III, no. 1065.
[36] Burckhardt-Biedermann, pp. 43–44.
[37] Hartmann, III, no. 1101.

however, a mounting tide of pressure on the part of the reform elements for the imposition of their discipline; the crisis was reached by Christmas 1528, when there began to be public disorders and rioting in the streets between rival factions. In January the evangelical mob stormed the churches and destroyed the images and on February 8, 1529, the council decreed the abolition of the mass. In April there was issued the reforming ordinance, with its provisions for the organization of public worship, which had been drawn up by Oecolampadius and naturally embodied his view of the sacrament of communion.[38]

The accomplishment of the successful revolution was the occasion for the departure from Basel of many of Amerbach's closest friends. The greatest loss was Erasmus who felt that he could no longer remain in a city which had officially adopted the doctrines of the Reform. He determined to go to Freiburg where he was offered imperial protection and where his and Boniface's old friend Zasius was still professor at the university. Oecolampadius and others endeavored to dissuade Erasmus but without success. He took his departure in April accompanied by a delegation of the council to wish him well.[39] Other friends like Ber had already preceded him. Now began a very difficult period for Amerbach; although he recognized that some good things had been accomplished, his sympathies were against the new order. On the other

---

[38] For a general account of the coming of the Reformation to Basel, see R. Wackernagel, *Geschichte der Stadt Basel* (Basel, 1924), III, 317–524. Two more recent studies are Paul Roth, *Die Reformation in Basel: Die Vorbereitungsjahre* (Basel, 1936) and *Die Durchführung der Reformation in Basel* (Basel, 1943).

[39] Allen, VIII, no. 2149.

hand his deep loyalty to the community, his family ties, and the administration of his property kept him in the city in spite of the temptations to join those friends who had gone into voluntary exile.

We can follow best in his constant correspondence with Erasmus the difficulties and indecisions of the years immediately following 1529. Boniface complains of the necessity for dissimulating his opinions, of the growth of factionalism, of the crimes committed in the name of evangelical liberty. In his more depressed moments he sees nothing good in prospect and compares living in Basel to living in Constantinople under the Turks.[40]

In this situation, notwithstanding the high esteem in which he was held, Amerbach could not long remain free of the pressure for conformity. In a series of steps taken during 1530 and 1531 Oecolampadius persuaded the council to adopt his views on the relation between ecclesiastical and political authority and to establish in each parish the *bannherrn,* three pious men, two from the council and one from the community, to collaborate with the pastor in maintaining surveillance over the orthodoxy of the parishioners and warning backsliders, who were to be first reported to the pastor and subsequently to the council. In April 1531 the council passed the edict *de non communicantibus* by which those who refused to accept the new order and absented themselves from the communion table were to be warned three times and then banished by the civil authority.[41]

---

[40] Allen, VIII, nos. 2199, 2219, 2223, 2224 (especially important for reflections on a sermon by Zwingli) and VIII, no. 2248.

[41] See the account in Burckhardt-Biedermann, pp. 78–130. Selections

Boniface had foreseen and dreaded these developments. A year before the council's edict he had written to Erasmus, "Oecolampadius by threat and terror leaves no stone unturned to bring the whole of Basel to his communion table." [42] Boniface had however hoped that his status as professor would give him exemption from the ordinances to conformity; this plea had earlier been recognized by the council and his fears that it might not be observed had been again expressed in letters to Erasmus.[43] By the spring of 1531 it was clear that there were to be no more exemptions in accordance with the terms of the edict of April, and Amerbach was summoned before the council. He requested a delay in which to prepare his views and on May 11th submitted to the council his prepared statement on why he rejected the communion of Oecolampadius.[44]

In this document, as a Christian he reiterates the principal articles of his creed and as a citizen he professes his pacific intentions and his obedience to the council. However on the interpretation of the eucharist he is uncompromising in rejecting the views of Oecolampadius. The words of the institution of the sacrament can mean only the real presence of the body and blood of Christ. They were not otherwise understood by antiquity and the whole history of the Church. He cannot believe that Christ would so long have left his Church in error. He doubts whether human reason can be applied to the mysteries of the faith and notes that disputation on these sub-

from Amerbach's diary are given on pp. 325–372. See also Allen, IX, no. 2519.

[42] Allen, VIII, no. 2312.

[43] See especially, Hartmann, III, no. 1405.

[44] This statement is printed in Hartmann, IV, nos. 470–476. See also Burckhardt-Biedermann, pp. 377–385.

jects which are beyond reason have often led to greater divisions rather than to greater unity. He has thoroughly studied and reflected and does not feel himself under the necessity of further instruction. Recalling the Marburg colloquy and the differences of opinion there expressed among the Reformers, he raises the question whether the council of Basel has not been inconsistent in entering into an alliance with the Saxons and Hessians who hold a different view of the eucharist from that of Oecolampadius while depriving citizens of Basel of their citizenship for the same reason.

Upon receipt of this document the council took no immediate action against their eminent professor. Basel under Oecolampadius was not what Geneva was to become under Calvin. Even the exchanges between those who were most uncompromisingly opposed on theological questions seem touched with the spirit of those pleas which had been uttered by Erasmus and Vadian on the value of considering opposing views.

Sometime in the weeks following his appearance before the council Boniface composed a letter to Luther. Perhaps, wrestling with his conscience, he recalled his earlier unqualified admiration for the Reformer and certainly he had reason to expect that Luther would support him against Oecolampadius on a doctrine of the real presence. It is questionable, however, whether this letter was ever sent since there exists no answer from Luther, and it is reasonable to suppose that in later discussion Boniface would have produced a document from such an authority if he had had one.[45]

[45] Burckhardt-Biedermann, pp. 87–88. The text of Boniface's letter is given in Hartmann, IV, no. 1533.

In subsequent appearances before the council, before the *bannherrn,* and in conversation with individual pastors including Oecolampadius himself, Boniface reiterated his position.[46] At the beginning of the acute phase of the controversy, in April 1531, he had written to his friend Montaigne in France that perhaps he would be forced to leave Basel but that he would do so rather than separate himself from an interpretation of the sacrament which had been the "communis ecclesiae consensus a tot seculis retro." [47]

In September 1531, after the ecclesiastical authorities had rendered an unfavorable report, Boniface was again summoned before the council. This time he requested a postponement until Easter but the council voted that he must conform and receive communion.[48] In spite of this vote, however, the authorities were still reluctant to act and the events of the war between the cantons, the battle of Cappel and the death of Zwingli created an atmosphere in which a final settlement could be further postponed. In fact though not in law, Boniface received the benefit of the delay for which he had petitioned. In the meantime his friends were divided between counselling firmness or concession. Zasius wrote to a third friend comparing Boniface's appearance before the council to that of St. Paul before Nero and rejoicing that Amerbach had not compromised.[49] His former roommate in Zasius's house in Freiburg wrote, however, in the opposite sense, urging

---

[46] See the diary in Burckhardt-Biedermann, pp. 325–372.
[47] Hartmann, IV, no. 1519.
[48] Burckhardt-Biedermann, p. 89.
[49] Hartmann, IV, no. 1574.

his friend to participate in the Christian life of the community.[50]

During this stormy period Boniface continued to note in his diary the events of the Swiss war and more than once revealed his sympathy with the Catholic cause.[51] The death of Oecolampadius on November 24th made it easier for the council to continue the policy of delay in the enforcement of conformity.

In the spring of 1532 Amerbach was invited to accept the professorship of civil law at the University of Dole in Burgundy.[52] This occasioned great indecision in Amerbach's mind and new negotiations with the council on the conditions on which he might remain in Basel. After a period of more than three months of consideration he refused the offer from Dole.[53] To Erasmus he confided that he had been much moved by family considerations, the reluctance of his wife and the opposition of his father-in-law, but he added that the magistrates had appealed to his sense of civic responsibility and his love for his fatherland.[54] The attitude of the council in this matter obviously made it difficult to proceed by legal action against a professor whom they had urged to continue in his post. Henceforth, persuasion rather than threats of compulsion were the means adopted to achieve Amerbach's acceptance of the religious order adopted by the community.

In the following year at Easter, on the occasion of new remonstrances against him, Boniface presented an addi-

[50] Hartmann, IV, no. 1566.
[51] See Burckhardt-Biedermann, p. 99, and the citations there given.
[52] Hartmann, IV, no. 1611.
[53] Hartmann, IV, no. 1640.
[54] Allen, IX, no. 2649.

tional statement in which he reiterated his belief in the real presence and his recognition that this miracle like other truths of divine revelation was beyond the comprehension of human reason.[55]

In January 1534 the council adopted the Basel confession of faith which had been drawn up by the successors of Oecolampadius. This was followed by an attempt of the pastor Phrygio, who was a friend of Boniface, to persuade him to accept this formulation and no longer separate himself from the religious life of the community.[56] Whether influenced by the arguments advanced by Phrygio or by the writing of the Strasburg Reformer, Martin Bucer, on the sacraments, which had begun to be circulated during this year,[57] Boniface found himself able to reconcile what he had previously regarded as irreconcilable. He submitted to the council his own *confessio fidei*[58] in which while again defending the doctrine of the real presence, he made clear that it was a question of "cibus animae non ventris" and of a union "non naturalis sed sacramentalis." He rejected the doctrine of the mass as a sacrifice and in his assertion of a real spiritual presence seems to anticipate the position of Calvin.[59] Following this confession Boniface began to attend religious services and receive communion according to the established

[55] Burckhardt-Biedermann, pp. 385–395.

[56] Hartmann, IV, no. 1802.

[57] Burckhardt-Biedermann, p. 102.

[58] This is printed in Hartmann, IV, no. 476–479, and in another version in Burckhardt-Biedermann, pp. 395–400. It is impossible to date this document accurately. See Hartmann, IV, no. 1803n for the convincing argument that it is not February 24, 1534.

[59] Calvin, *Petit Traicté de la sainte cene,* in *Opera omnia,* G. Baum, E. Cunitz, and E. Reuss, eds., 59 vols. (Brunschweig, 1863–1900), V, 429–460.

order, thus ending his alienation from his fellow-citizens and at the same time marking his formal acceptance of the Reformation. However decisive this step may have seemed to him it did not cost him the sympathy and support of the large circle of friends in the Catholic world with whom he remained in unbroken correspondence.

In 1535, with harmony between himself and the council restored, Amerbach became a syndic of that governing body while continuing his professorship of civil law at the university. In that same year the aged Erasmus returned to Basel from Freiburg ostensibly for the purpose of seeing through the press his latest works, the edition of Origen and the *Ecclesiastes*. He was installed in Froben's house and it soon became clear he was too ill to make any further journey. There, attended by Boniface and others of his closest friends and admirers, he died on July 12, 1536. Amerbach was named as his principal heir and together with Nicholas Episcopius and Hieronymus Froben, assumed the obligation of administering the considerable wealth left by Erasmus to be used for charitable purposes.[60] A large portion of the income of these trusts was applied to the establishment of scholarships at the University of Basel.[61]

In spite of the many commitments consequent upon his public responsibilities and the private practice of his profession,[62] Amerbach continued to maintain the intel-

---

[60] The most recent account of the death of Erasmus with full bibliography is contained in C. Reedijk, "Das Lebensende des Erasmus," *Basler Zeitschrift für Geschichte und Altertumskunde* 57:23–66 (1958). Erasmus's last will is given in Allen, XI, appendix XXV.

[61] Allen, XI, appendix XXV.

[62] Alfred Hartmann, "Bonifacius Amerbach als Verwalter der Eras-

lectual and artistic interests that had made his name so well-known not only in Basel but in the European world of letters. His knowledge of the history and literature of Greece and Rome was encyclopedic and he followed with eagerness the discovery of additional manuscripts and the appearance of new editions of classical authors. He had befriended the musician Hans Kotter, organist in Freiburg.[63] He continued the collection of manuscripts, coins, and works of art, including the famous Holbeins which formed the nucleus of the Amerbach *kabinett* and ultimately passed to the possession of his native city.[64] His family life appears to have been singularly happy and in his later years he had the satisfaction of seeing his surviving children happily married and his son prepared to maintain both the intellectual and professional interests of the family tradition. Throughout the whole of his life he vigorously carried on with his many friends abroad the enormous correspondence which provides so unique a documentation of the intellectual history of his generation. He died on April 24, 1562, a man whose piety and learning were respected by Catholic and Protestant alike, an exemplar of moderation and charity in an age of violence.

In the critical decisions of both his professional and his religious life Boniface Amerbach showed himself to

---

mus-stiftung," *Basler Jahrbuch* (1957), pp. 7–28. See also Guido Kisch, "Bonifacius Amerbach als Rechtsgutachter," *Festgabe zum siebsigten Geburstag von Max Gerwig* (Basel, 1960), pp. 85–120.

[63] W. Merian, "Bonifacius Amerbach und Hans Kotter," *Basler Zeitschrift für Geschichte* 16:140–206 (1917).

[64] P. Ganz and E. Major, *Die Entstehung des Amerbachschen Kunstkabinetts und die Amerbachschen Inventare* (Basel, 1907).

be a conservative. The law ought not to be taught without due attention to the commentaries, that is, to the history of what it has meant to succeeding generations. Religious doctrine ought not to embrace such innovation as would set aside the universal practice of the Church in past centuries. Yet, in these decisions and attitudes on law and theology, there is more than a mere temperamental reaction against certain kinds of changes; in Boniface's thought there can be distinguished at least the elements of what may be called a philosophy of history.

His view of history is characteristically revealed in the attack on the grammarians, those who try to "explain the code as if it were a comedy of Plautus or Terence." The Italian humanists had endowed grammatical and philological studies with extraordinary prestige. The greatest scholars of their age like Valla and Poliziano had begun the application of these methods to the understanding of legal texts. Amerbach himself had profited by the further development of these methods especially at the hands of his great teacher Alciato. Nevertheless when he saw such a professor as Sichard justifying the grammatical analysis of the original text to the complete exclusion of the medieval commentators he felt that the reaction had gone too far. The original critics of the glossators and post-glossators and of the scholastic theologians had maintained that they were ignorant of history. In pleading the cause of a return to the original sources they felt they were defending historical truth against dogmatic and unhistorical distortions. A more sophisticated view, however, recognized the limitations of a purely grammatical exegesis. In attacking such men as Sichard in law and

Oecolampadius in theology, Boniface is not advocating an unhistorical approach to the study of these subjects; on the contrary he recognizes the contributions to historical *knowledge* made by humanist scholarship. He maintains, in effect, that we cannot have historical *understanding* by skipping over the centuries intervening between the present and antiquity whether classic or Christian. His position, which in legal studies represented a synthesis of the *mos italicus* and the *mos gallicus,* may thus be seen as a defense of history against those who were themselves self-consciously using the weapons of the new historical and philological criticism in their controversy with the Bartolists. Texts like the code of the civil law and the Bible, which had been inextricably intertwined with the history of human institutions, could not be understood by neglecting history, that is to say, neglecting the series of commentators and concentrating on the grammatical meaning alone.[65]

Amerbach's view of history was closely connected with his conception of the principle of equity. The infinite variety of situations which occurred in the course of human history imposed the necessity of adapting the norms of religious and legal traditions to the circumstances rather than attempting in every case a strict and legal application of a rule. In his *Defensio interpretum iuris civilis* Boniface is concerned to point out that, although the commentators do not make new law, they rely on the sources of law, the responses of the jurisconsults, and the constitutions of the emperors, to furnish a kind of Lesbian rule to be applied to the infinite realm

[65] See the discussion on pp. 35–37.

of fact in accordance with the changing circumstances.[66]
He here refers to the *Nicomachean Ethics* where Aristotle
speaks of the flexible measure adapted by the Lesbians
to the character of their architecture.[67] Professor Kisch
has pointed out the significance of this statement and in
his comprehensive analysis has established Boniface Amerbach's place in the evolution of a conception of equity.[68]
It is interesting that in his discussion of the religious question Boniface uses the same terminology. In a letter to
Montaigne of 1524 he speaks again of the Lesbian norm
and demands to know why those who have in charge the
affairs of the church cannot adapt the decrees of men to
the purpose of the Evangel.[69] The expression had been
popularized by Erasmus who had included it in his
Adages, where a Lesbian rule is described as an accommodation of reason to fact rather than fact to reason, or an
adaptation of the law to mores rather than the mores to
the law.[70]

In his early years Boniface had quoted another adage
from Erasmus "veritas filia temporis." [71] This remark of
Aulus Gellius had enjoyed a certain popularity in the
Renaissance and was adopted and reinterpreted by the
Protestant Reformers as well as by later generations.[72] To
Boniface in the years when he entertained the highest

[66] Hartmann, III, appendix I, p. 556, lines 70–80.

[67] Aristotle, *Nicomachean Ethics,* bk. V, ch. x.

[68] Kisch, *Erasmus und die Jurisprudenz,* pp. 344–380.

[69] Hartmann, II, no. 962.

[70] Erasmus, *Adagiorum chiliades* (Hanover, 1617), p. 43.

[71] Erasmus, *ibid.,* p. 362. For the expression as used by Boniface, cf.
Hartmann, II, no. 686.

[72] F. Saxl, "Veritas filia Temporis," in *Philosophy and History: Essays
Presented to Ernst Cassirer* (Oxford, 1936), pp. 197–222.

hopes of the Reformation, when he could still believe that Erasmus and Luther were working together for a restoration of theology that would parallel the restoration already achieved in law and medicine, this expression seems to imply a sudden revelation of the truth. In a letter to his brother he also uses the metaphor of Truth laying aside the mask and at last showing her true countenance.[73] Holbein painted his celebrated portrait of Amerbach in 1519. Boniface was then twenty-four years old and had just returned from Freiburg to Basel. It was the moment of his most generous enthusiasm for the intellectual and spiritual revolution of which he felt that Luther and Erasmus were the leaders; his generation would be privileged to confront a world in which Truth would be revealed. Holbein, who was two years younger than Amerbach and shared the same hopes, has conveyed in the portrait of his friend the quality of this steady confidence in the future. But the moment passed. With the experience of the intellectual and religious conflicts through which he lived in the decade from 1525 to 1535 Amerbach came to have a different and a more sober view of the relation between Time and Truth. Nearly forty years after he was painted by Holbein we have his portrait by Jacob Clauser in 1557.[74] Here is the syndic of the council, the university professor, the administrator of Erasmus's trusts. For him there will be no sudden revelation. If Truth is to be wrested from Time it will be by careful study of the tradition of what men have thought and said in every age on the great legal and moral prob-

[73] Hartmann, II, no. 746.
[74] Reproduced in Kisch, *Erasmus und die Jurisprudenz,* p. 352.

BONIFACE AMERBACH, BY HANS HOLBEIN (1519)

BONIFACE AMERBACH, BY JACOB CLAUSNER (1557)

lems. "Ex variarum opinionum collatione . . . quid veritati magis consentianeum elicietur." On propositions given by divine revelation beyond the capacity of human reason to understand, disputation may lead to disunity, but in all those complicated attempts that men must make to adapt to varying circumstances the rules of law and the rules of the Evangel, the attainment of Truth will be a slow process, the product of a continuing dialogue from which there cannot be excluded the voices of the past.

INDEX

INDEX

❧❦

Abelard, Pierre, 40
Accolti, Francesco, 70
Accursius, Franciscus, 62, 157
Achilles, 96
Albert of Mainz, 160n
Alberti, Leon Battista, 11, 39, 40
Alciato, Andrea, 66, 85, 147, 151, 153, 161, 163, 173; early works and method, 32–34; on monasticism, 79–82; on post-glossators, 155–157
Alcibiades, 45, 89
Alcuin, 124
Aleander, Jerome, 132, 138
Alexander the Great, 90, 96
Alexander VI, 51, 71
Alfonso the Magnanimous, King of Naples, 43, 45
Allegretti, Allegreto, 68n
Altilius, Giovanni, 44, 45
Amerbach, Basil, 154
Amerbach, Boniface, 82, 85, 118, 119, 133, 139, 144; correspondence with Erasmus (1530–1535), 126–128; character, 146–147; background and early education, 148–150; further studies, 151–154; on teaching law, 155–160; on the Reformation, 161–171; conservative idea of history, 172–177
Amerbach, Johannes (or Hans), 148, 149, 150
Andromache, 95
Aretino, Pietro, 39, 40
Aristotle, 16, 45, 90, 97, 128, 175
Atticus, Titus Pomponius, 12
Augustus (of Rome), 90

Bartolus of Sassoferrato, 29, 79; attacked by humanists, 31–34, 36, 62–64, 69, 159–160; defended by Amerbach, 154–155, 157
Bayle, Pierre, 116
Bembo, Pietro, 103
Ber, Louis, 120, 121, 130, 162, 163, 164
Berruguete, Pedro, 24
Berquin, Louis, 139
Bisticci, Vespasiano da, 24, 25n
Blarer, Thomas, 161
Boccaccio, Giovanni, 30
Bodin, Jean, 85; *Methodus,* 34–37; idea of history, 56–58
Boeza, Hector, life of Decio, 66n, 73n, 77n
Borgia, Cesare, 67
Bracciolini, Poggio, 30, 39
Briçonnet, Guillaume, 48
Bruni, Leonardo, 20, 21, 30, 136, 158n
Brutus, Marcus Junius, 14
Bucer, Martin, 122, 123, 138, 170
Budé, Guillaume, 32, 85, 151
Buonarroti, Michelangelo, 11
Burke, Edmund, 61
Bussi, Giovanni Andrea, Bishop of Aleria, 23, 25

Caesar, Julius, 89, 96, 139
Calvin, John, 67, 85, 139, 167, 170
Camillus, Marcus Furius, 14
Camp, Victor, 159
Cantiuncula, Claudius, 155, 156, 162
Capito, Wolfgang, 123, 160n

[181]

INDEX

INDEX

INDEX

*The type used in this book
is an old-style face known as
Linotype Granjon.*

*It was designed by the English printer,
George W. Jones.*

*Composed and printed
by the Crimson Printing Company
of Cambridge, Massachusetts,
and bound by the Stanhope Bindery, Inc.,
of Boston.*

*Book design by David Ford
of the Harvard University Press.*